THEIR GILDED CAGE

THE JEKYLL ISLAND CLUB MEMBERS

By Richard Jay Hutto
Preface by Stillman Rockefeller
Introduction by June Hall McCash

Henchard Press Ltd.

Publisher	Henry S. Beers
Associate Publisher	Richard J. Hutto
Executive Vice President	Robert G. Aldrich
Operations Manager	Gary G. Pulliam
Editor-in-Chief	Joni Woolf
Art Director/Designer	Julianne Gleaton
Designer	Daniel Emerson
Director of Marketing and Public Relations	Mary D. Robinson

Printed in India.

Library of Congress Control Number: 2005936795

ISBN: (10 digit) 0-9770912-2-8
          (13 digit) 978-0-9770912-2-5

Endpaper sketch and palm frond art used throughout were drawn at Jekyll Island by Mrs. J. P. Morgan, Jr. (Jane Norton) and are used through the generosity of the Archives of The Pierpont Morgan Library, New York.

Henchard Press Ltd. books are available at quantity discounts
with bulk purchase for educational, business, or sales promotional use.
For information, please write to:
Henchard Press Ltd., SunTrust Bank Building, 435 Second St. Suite 320, Macon, GA 31201, or call 866-311-9578.
www.henchardpress.com

"IF YOU COULD ONLY SEE IT ALL! IT SEEMS LIKE A RARE COLLECTION OF VERY HIGH BRED AND EXCLUSIVE ANIMALS ... ENJOYING THEIR GILDED CAGE VERY MUCH."

Kate Brown, tutor to the Valentine Macy children, describing in a letter her first impressions of the Jekyll Island Club.

The Carnegie family at Cumberland Island.

PREFACE

My family and I share a long-standing love affair with Georgia's coast. Two of my great-great-grandfathers, James Stillman and William Rockefeller, were early members of the Jekyll Island Club while the family of my other great-great-grandparents, Lucy and Thomas Carnegie, owned Cumberland Island. In fact, I am one of the few Carnegie family members who still own a home on Cumberland and spend part of each year there.

The same beauty and serenity that brought our family to Georgia's coast, however, is constantly under threat. That is why we continue to remain committed to protecting Cumberland's natural resources. The same is true of Jekyll where, by law, sixty-five percent of the Island must remain undeveloped. I applaud the work of the Jekyll Island Foundation to protect a natural habitat that cannot be replaced, and to teach a new generation their responsibilities as guardians of this magical place. As you read about the men and women who banded together more than a century ago to enjoy Jekyll, I hope you will help us to honor them by being good stewards of their legacy.

Stillman Rockefeller

INTRODUCTION

When the *New York Times* announced on April 4, 1886, the founding of the Jekyll Island Club, off the coast of Brunswick, Georgia, the reporter predicted that it would be "the 'swell' club, the crème de la crème of all." Almost twenty years later, *Munsey's Magazine* suggested that it had fulfilled that prediction, calling it "the richest, the most exclusive, the most inaccessible" club in the world. In fact, its membership roster was like a "Who's Who" of the late nineteenth and early twentieth centuries. Names like Rockefeller, Vanderbilt, Morgan, Astor, Gould, Pulitzer, Bliss, Auchincloss, and Goelet were common at the Club. Many of them were household names equivalent to wealth in the minds of average Americans. All would have been well recognized in New York and Chicago society. But Jekyll Island Club members were more than merely wealthy. They were, by and large, people who made monumental and lasting contributions to American society and not only in the business world, where many of them obviously thrived. There were bankers, merchants, engineers, inventors,

architects, physicians, lawyers, clergymen, congressmen, senators, and ambassadors. They were also vital civic and cultural leaders, reformers, and philanthropists of the first order. Without their contributions to American society—to universities, museums, art galleries, hospitals, and organizations like the Red Cross and the Boy and Girl Scouts, our nation would today be culturally poorer.

There can be little question that the club's success surpassed even the wildest dreams of its founders, who sought to bring wealthy New Yorkers and Chicagoans south for hunting at magnificent Jekyll Island during the winter. Newton Finney, who is credited with the founding of the club, was at the time living in New York and a member of the so called "mother of clubs," New York's Union Club. Although from Wisconsin himself, he had served in the Confederacy during the Civil War, having in 1860 married a young woman from Brunswick, Georgia, Josephine du Bignon, whose family members had been ardent secessionists. They had also owned Jekyll Island for almost a century. When the War and Reconstruction had ended, her brother, John Eugene du Bignon, a New South entrepreneur, was determined, like his brother-in-law Finney, to regain the fortune he had lost during the War, and set out to re-acquire Jekyll Island, which family members had sold off in parcels during the tribulations of post-war Georgia. With the help of New Yorker John Claflin and an investment of only $13,000, he succeeded in his plan. In turn, the newly-formed Jekyll Island Club, organized by Finney, purchased the island for $125,000, constructed a fine clubhouse, and opened for its first season in 1888.

In many respects the club was unique. Its location not only in the South, but on a secluded island off the Georgia coast was unusual. It provided a family winter haven that, in terms of ambiance, fell somewhere between the elite atmosphere of Newport and the rustic camps of the Adirondacks. In fact, it began as a hunting club, though from the outset it welcomed and provided for the needs of entire families. As years went on, activities like tennis and golf took on greater importance. The club changed with the times, as its members' interests reflect. But one thing that remained constant was the desire of club families to enjoy the natural wonders of the island. Although they quickly embraced the Great Bicycle Craze and built bike paths through the forests, they were much less eager to accept the noisy intrusion of the automobile. After much debate, in 1900, the executive committee finally allowed the unwelcome vehicles on the island,

though strictly limited their hours of operation from 10:00 a.m. to noon and from 2:00 p.m. to 7:00 p.m. They were permitted only on the beach and back roads and to speeds of six miles an hour and had to stop completely when meeting horses, driven or ridden. In short, they were never the favored mode of transportation at Jekyll.

Almost immediately after the club's opening, some of the members, who had received a lot with every two shares of club stock (which was limited to 100 shares), began almost at once to build houses for their families, creating what club members referred to informally as the "Cottage Colony." Some families spent the entire club season, from January until April, on the island. Others came for briefer stays. But the mild winter weather and the spectacular springs, the sunsets over the marshes, and the gentle seas welcomed them throughout the season.

When one reads of the careers of the Jekyll Island Club members, male and female, outlined in this book, one can imagine the extraordinary conversations that took place and the ideas and plans that were born in the clubhouse parlors or on its wide veranda. In fact, Dr. Walter Belknap James, who was club president during the 1920s, once commented that the "real core in Jekyll Island's great days was to be found in the men's after dinner talks. It was always of great things, of visions and developing. If they didn't have a map of the United States before them, they had a map of industrial or financial empires in their minds." Even today, there is scarcely any aspect of modern business and economics that they did not impact in some important way.

More than one person who can still remember visiting the island as a child during the club era still refer to it as "heaven on earth." Such memories are not surprising when one considers the childhood magic of an overnight train ride that departed from New York in the snows and allowed one to awaken the next morning to the palm trees and gentle sea breezes of the Georgia coast. Children enjoyed carriage rides on the beach, bicycling along the narrow paths that cut through the island's unspoiled center, swimming in the middle of winter in the Goulds' swimming pool, and later at the pool built in front of the club house in 1927. They loved the beach activities like picnics, shelling, and the races of the "redbugs," motorized go-carts developed to discourage the use of automobiles. Like their parents and grandparents, children enjoyed the family time, the birdsong, and the Spanish moss that graced the live oak trees. When all had been cold and barren in the northern winter, at Jekyll the Cherokee roses and the camellias were in bloom.

Inevitably, over time the club evolved and changed. National and world events took their toll: the Great Depression, World War I, and a general decline of interest in the Victorian atmosphere of Jekyll in favor of other resorts like those in Florida and at Sea Island designed by Addison Mizner, or the spas and cities of Europe, which became increasingly popular with people of means after World War I. The club was already in decline by the time World War II began. After the bombing of Pearl Harbor in December 1941, the club held only one more season, which ended in early April 1942. The war effort required the manpower, the resources, and the transportation systems on which the Jekyll Island Club had depended to provide for its members' needs and desires. Shortly after the season ended, German submarines torpedoed a vessel in Brunswick harbor. The war had reached the very waters in which Joseph Pulitzer, J. P. Morgan, and George Fisher Baker, among others, had sailed their yachts during their trips to Jekyll.

The state of Georgia took over the island in 1947, and in recent years, the magnificent club house has been restored and reopened as a splendid hotel. Most of the cottages built or owned by the Rockefellers, the Goodyears, the Macys, and the Goulds are still standing. Two of them, Crane Cottage, owned by the family of Richard Teller Crane, and Cherokee, built by Edwin Gould for his in-laws and later purchased by Dr. and Mrs. Walter James while he was club president, have opened as bed-and-breakfast extensions of the club house hotel. The grounds have been restored to their former splendor, and descendants of former club members have begun to rediscover Jekyll's charm and to hold family reunions on the island. Once again, the Jekyll Island Club is the center of activity for the magnificent and unique historic district of the island. Once again, descendants of club families can enjoy the splendid bike paths, high tea at the club house, and the magnificent sunsets over the Marshes of Glynn. Jekyll Island has well earned its reputation as "Georgia's Jewel," and it still welcomes those who come today to enjoy its natural beauty, where sixty-five per cent of the island must remain undeveloped according to state law. Today, we can all enjoy the wonders of the island that were once reserved only for the privileged few, those extraordinary club members whose stories are told in this volume.

June Hall McCash, PhD.,
Author of The Jekyll Island Cottage Colony, and Jekyll Island's Early Years:
From Prehistory through Reconstruction. Co-Author of The Jekyll Island
Club: Southern Haven for America's Millionaires.

Tea at Mistletoe Cottage, Jekyll Island, 1910

THEIR GILDED CAGE

THE JEKYLL ISLAND CLUB MEMBERS

JOHN JOSEPH ALBRIGHT (1848 – 1931), financier and philanthropist. With his partner, Jekyll Island Club (JIC) member General Edmund B. Hayes, he brought the Lackawanna Steel Company's plant to Buffalo and was a pioneer in the development of Niagara Falls water power in New York State and Canada. In 1901 he gave the Albright Art Gallery to the City of Buffalo (at a cost of $1 million) and also donated a library to his boyhood home in Scranton, Pennsylvania. Albright was one of the incorporators of the American Academy in Rome and was a brother-in-law of JIC member Amzi L. Barber (their wives were sisters) with whom he was a partner in developing Washington's LeDroit Park area. Albright's step-grandson was the husband of the first female U. S. Secretary of State, Madeleine Albright.

NELSON WILMARTH ALDRICH (1841- 1915), banker and senator. Formerly a street railway developer and Wall Street partner, Aldrich served four terms in the U.S. Senate from Rhode Island. As chairman of the Senate Finance Committee he wrote the gold standard act of 1900 and was a proponent of protectionism. In 1910 he secretly led a group meeting at Jekyll Island to devise what would eventually become the Federal Reserve System. Aldrich's daughter, Abby, married John D. Rockefeller, Jr. and their grandson is current U. S. Senator John D. Rockefeller, IV. Another Aldrich grandson was U. S. Vice President Nelson Aldrich Rockefeller, whose father-in-law was JIC member Edward White Clark.

WINTHROP WILLIAMS ALDRICH (1885 – 1974) attorney, banker and diplomat. A son of JIC member Nelson W. Aldrich, he served as U. S. Ambassador to the Court of St. James from 1953 to 1957. His wife was a daughter of prominent attorney Charles B. Alexander and a granddaughter of San Francisco banker Charles Crocker. Aldrich was decorated for his services by the governments of England, Belgium, France, the Netherlands, and the Vatican. He was president of the Rockefeller-controlled Chase National Bank of New York.

SAMUEL WATERS ALLERTON (1828 - 1914), capitalist and meatpacker. Allerton was an early financier of the stockyards of East St. Louis and eventually owned more than ten thousand acres along the Sangamon River near Monticello, Illinois. He was also a founder of the Chicago stockyards and of the First National Bank of Chicago. His son, Robert, built the palatial Allerton House and eventually gave it to the University of Illinois at Urbana-Champaign as a conference and nature center. Allerton also had a summer resort at Lake Geneva, Wisconsin, and a winter home in California. His daughter, Kate, was the wife of JIC member Hugo R. Johnstone and became the Club's first female member.

WILLIAM POPE ANDERSON (1874 – 1951), engineer. Anderson organized and became president of the Ferro Concrete Construction Company of Cincinnati and built the nation's first concrete non-steel enforced skyscraper there.

AVERY DeLANO ANDREWS (1864 - 1959), attorney. Andrews served as a Brigadier General and was chief of staff to General Pershing in France in 1918. Decorated by the governments of France, Belgium, and Italy, he wrote *My Friend and Classmate,*

Left: John Albright and daughter Nancy at their Jekyll home purchased from Joseph Pulitzer.

Top: Allerton House near Monticello, Illinois.

Right: Senator Nelson Aldrich who led a group at Jekyll to organize what would become the Federal Reserve System.

Left: John J. Astor IV in costume for the Bradley Martin Ball of 1897. He perished on the Titanic but his much-younger pregnant wife survived. She eventually married JIC member William K. Dick.

Right: Vincent Astor (in bowler hat) with his mother, Lady Ribblesdale.

John J. Pershing. His wife, Mary, was a daughter of Lt. General John M. Schofield.

BENJAMIN WALWORTH ARNOLD (1865 - 1932), banker and industrialist. A resident of Albany, New York, Arnold was president of the Duluth and Northern Minnesota Railroad. A respected ornithologist, Arnold was married three times and widowed twice.

LLOYD ASPINWALL (1830- 1886), shipping executive. He was a son of William H. Aspinwall, whose mother was a Howland, thus uniting New York City's two largest shipping families. Howland and Aspinwall were pioneers in quick transportation across Panama and had the largest Pacific trade of any firm in New York, besides doing an extensive business with the East and West Indies, England, and the Mediterranean. The family firm secured the contract for a line of mail steamers from the Isthmus of Panama to California, as well as a concession from the government of New Granada for the construction of a railroad across the isthmus. The road was completed after many difficulties and opened on 17 February 1855, the eastern terminus being named Aspinwall (now Colon). Lloyd Aspinwall was General Burnside's aide at Fredericksburg, and after the war was a brigadier general in the 4th New York Brigade. He was a director of the Mexican National Railroad and served as the first president of the Jekyll Island Club but died five months into his term. His sister, Anna Lloyd Aspinwall, married JIC member James Renwick. Their father's sister, Mary Rebecca Aspinwall, married Isaac Roosevelt and was the grandmother of Franklin Delano Roosevelt. Aspinwall was also a brother-in-law of JIC member William Bradford D'Wolf. In 1886 JIC member William Rockefeller became interested in extensive property owned by Lloyd Aspinwall and purchased it for $150,000, turning the property into his Hudson River estate, "Rockwood Hall." Aspinwall's granddaughter, Bessie, married Ralph Pulitzer, Jr., son of a JIC member.

LLOYD ASPINWALL, JR. (JIC member 1886-1892), shipping executive. Son of the JIC's first president, he served as treasurer of the Club in 1888. In 1882 he married Cornelia Sutton and, when she divorced him in 1893, her charges were thought so sensitive that the court sealed the legal papers. His gambling debts became so extensive that he forged his brother's signature on a $2,400 note drawn on their family business and was ultimately jailed. He testified that he had neither home nor money at the time of his arrest and was denied bail. At his death in 1899, the *New York Times* wrote, "One-Time Well-Known and Wealthy Clubman Dies in Comparative Poverty."

WILLIAM VINCENT ASTOR (1891 – 1959), financier and yachtsman. Vincent was the son of John Jacob and legendary beauty Ava Willing Astor (later Lady Ribblesdale). When his father died on the *Titanic,* he inherited $87 million and took over the family business at the age of twenty-one. Vincent was a grandson of the social arbiter known as "the" Mrs. Astor and the brother of Princess Serge Obolensky. After his parents divorced, his forty-seven-year-old father shocked society by marrying Madeleine Force, who was younger than Vincent. The senior Astors cut short their honeymoon to return on the *Titanic* when she was determined

Top: Henry M. Atkinson, founder of the Georgia Power Company, in front of a power plant named in his honor.

Bottom: John J. Astor IV with Madeleine Force who was to become his second wife. She was younger than his son, JIC member Vincent Astor.

to be pregnant. Madeleine was left a wealthy young widow but no financial provision had been made for her child at the time of his father's death. She later married JIC member William Karl Dick, chairman of the National Sugar Refining Company (his father was also a JIC member), relinquished all claims to the Astor fortune, and had two more sons. Vincent Astor owned *Newsweek* magazine and turned over his yacht, the *Nourmahal*, to the government for use during both world wars. Although married three times, Vincent had no children and his fortune established the Vincent Astor Foundation headed by his last wife, philanthropist and socialite Brooke Astor. Vincent's home was "Ferncliff" in Rhinebeck, New York.

HENRY MORRELL ATKINSON (1862 – 1939), power company president. Atkinson founded Atlanta's first electric street car company; organized the Atlanta, Birmingham and Atlantic Railway; and in 1891 established Georgia Electric Light which became the Georgia Power Company. He and his wife, a daughter of Col. Richard Peters of Atlanta, lived there and at "The Birches" in Canada. His son-in-law, Jackson Dick, was an officer at Georgia Power Company.

GORDON AUCHINCLOSS (1886 - 1943), attorney. He served as secretary to his father-in-law, Col. Edward M. House, who was a close advisor to President Woodrow Wilson during the Peace Conference in Paris in 1919. His maternal grandfather, Samuel Sloan, was president of the Delaware, Lackawanna & Western Railroad and of the Hudson River Railroad. Auchincloss' brother, Reginald, married Ruth Cutting, daughter of JIC member William Bayard

Cutting. Auchincloss' descendant and namesake was the chief prosecutor of singer Michael Jackson in his 2005 California trial.

EMMA BURR JENNINGS AUCHINCLOSS (Mrs. Hugh Dudley Auchincloss) (born 1861; JIC member 1932-42), philanthropist. A daughter of Oliver Burr Jennings and Esther Judson Goodsell Jennings, her mother's sister was the wife of JIC member William Rockefeller. Her father was an early merchant in the California gold rush and eventually owned ten percent of Standard Oil. His business partner was Benjamin Brewster who was to head Standard Oil's export business. Brewster's daughter, Mary, married Jennings' son, Oliver Gould, and their son, Benjamin Brewster Jennings, eventually presided over Mobil Oil. Emma and her siblings were descended from U. S. Vice President Aaron Burr. In 1891 she married financier Hugh D. Auchincloss (1858-1913) and their son married as his second wife Janet Lee Bouvier, mother of Jacqueline Kennedy Onassis, and lived at "Merrywood" in McLean, Virginia. It was at Hammersmith Farm, the Auchincloss' home in Newport, that Jackie married future President John F. Kennedy. Emma and her brother, Oliver Gould Jennings, and their sister contributed funds to restore the Fairfield, Connecticut, town hall in 1939. Emma's daughter, Esther, married Reno casino pioneer Norman Blitz who was known as "the Duke of Nevada."

WILLIAM LISETER AUSTIN (1852 – 1932), engineer and inventor. He was a locomotive manufacturer who was awarded the gold medal for locomotive designs at the Paris Exposition of 1900. He eventually sold his interests to Baldwin Locomotive Works in 1911 and became the company's chairman. Austin was a member of the Union League Club and in 1877 married Mary Rogers of Philadelphia.

HOPE NORMAN BACON (Mrs. Elliott Cowdin Bacon/ Mrs. Paul E. Gardner) (JIC member 1930-37). A daughter of Guy Norman, she married Elliott Cowdin Bacon, the second youngest partner at J. P. Morgan & Company and a son of U. S. Secretary of State and Ambassador to France Robert Bacon. Elliot C. Bacon died in 1924 and she then married Paul Edgerton Gardner, a stockbroker at Farnum, Winter Company of Chicago, who died in 1938. Her son by her first marriage married Marjorie Goodyear, daughter of JIC member Frank H. Goodyear, Jr. Frederick Law Olmsted designed her burial plot at St. John's Memorial Cemetery.

MARTHA WALDRON COWDIN BACON (Mrs. Robert Bacon) (JIC member from 1926; died 1940). A daughter of Elliot C. Cowdin, in 1883 she married Robert Bacon (1860 – 1919), banker and diplomat. After serving as a partner at J. P. Morgan & Company, he was named Secretary of State in 1909 by President Theodore Roosevelt, then Ambassador to France from 1909 to 1912 in the Taft administration. They lived at "Old Acres" in Westbury, Long Island. Among their children were Congressman Robert Low Bacon; lieutenant governor of Massachusetts, Gaspar Griswold Bacon; Elliot Cowdin Bacon, whose wife was a JIC member; and Martha, whose husband was JIC member George Whitney, chairman of the board of J. P. Morgan & Co.

FRANCES EMMA STEERS LAKE BAKER (Mrs. Frederic Baker) (JIC member from 1897; died 1919). A daughter of James R. Steers, she was the widow of dry goods merchant George Graham

Lake and had two children when she met and married Frederic Baker while he was in his fifties. They had one daughter, Abigail, who died as a child and Baker reared his step-children as his own. She became a member of the Club in her own right in 1897 and visited without her husband when he was indisposed. She became the patron of a public school built on the Island for children of the Club's employees and was known for her generosity throughout the year. On March 9, 1914, "Solterra," their Jekyll home, caught fire and burned to the ground although many of its furnishings were saved by the Club's employees. She vowed to rebuild but never did and, on the site of "Solterra," the Crane family would later build the Club's grandest home.

FREDERIC BAKER (1831 - 1913), dry goods partner. President of the dry goods firm Baker and Williams, he and his family lived on Fifth Avenue in New York City and had a summer home in Southampton. In 1891 he built what was, up till then, the largest house at Jekyll, which he called "Solterra." From 1889 to 1908 Baker served as treasurer of the JIC, was instrumental in building Faith Chapel on the Island, and was a close associate of Henry Hyde in expanding the Club. While the Bakers were away in Europe and Africa in 1899, their home at Jekyll was used to host U. S. President McKinley at the invitation of JIC member Cornelius N. Bliss. Also present on Jekyll at the time was the vice president, the Speaker of the U. S. House of Representatives, and their respective wives. When Baker died at his New York City home, he left generous bequests both to the Club and to its resident manager.

GEORGE FISHER BAKER (1840 – 1931), banker. Founder of the First National Bank of New York, at his death the *New York Times* called him "Dean of the Nation's Bankers." Baker gave away millions of dollars in philanthropy and had a summer residence, "Imlagh," at Tuxedo Park. He married Florence Tucker, who died in 1913. Their son, George, Jr., inherited $60 million at his father's death and died in 1937 of peritonitis aboard his yacht, the *Viking*, in Honolulu. The senior Baker celebrated his ninetieth birthday at Jekyll, hosting a dinner for sixty people aboard his yacht. His only sister married JIC member Grant Barney Schley, and his grandson and namesake, George Baker St. George, was a JIC member.

JOHN HERBERT BALLANTINE (1867-1946), manufacturer. Ballantine was chairman of the board of Neptune Meter Company in Newark and lived at "Holmdene" in Great Neck, Long Island. After the death in 1919 of his first wife, Lois Wilgus, whom he wed in 1890, he married Gertrude W. Drake.

AMZI LORENZO BARBER (1843 – 1909), contractor. President of the Barber Asphalt Pavement Company, he secured from Great Britain a forty-two-year lease of the Pitch Lake in Trinidad, consisting of one hundred and fourteen acres of pitch asphalt. Barber lived in Washington, D.C., with a summer home in Staten Island that was formerly the Cunard home. His second wife was Julia Louise Langdon, daughter of John LeDroit Langdon, for whom Washington's LeDroit Park area was named. They lived at "Belmont" in Washington and at "Ardsley Towers" in Ardsley-on-Hudson, New York. He was a brother-in-law of JIC member John J. Albright (their wives were sisters) with whom he developed LeDroit Park in Washington. Barber was one of the founders of Howard

Top: George F. Baker and his son, George, Jr., leaving the Congressional Office Building.

Bottom: Solterra Cottage, the home of Frederic Baker, on fire at Jekyll in 1914. Servants and Club employees saved what they could but the home was a total loss.

Above: James J. Hill flanked by Morgan partner Charles Steele and George F. Baker on the right, 1910

Left: Francis Bartow, Jr., in a four-wheeled sailing vehicle on the beach at Jekyll, 1938.

Above: Dr. Lewellys Barker, who wrote in 1942 his memoirs of a distinguished life in medicine.

University where he taught philosophy but, at his second marriage, he resigned his post at Howard. His house, "Belmont," bounded by 13th and 14th Streets and Florida Avenue, gave its name to Washington's Belmont Street. Barber was a trustee of Oberlin College, where he earned his undergraduate and masters degrees. An art collector and yachtsman, Barber sailed with his family through the Mediterranean from Gibraltar to Constantinople in 1893-4.

ALEXANDER BARING (JIC member 1888-1898; died 1952). His wife, Louise Thorne King, was a daughter of Edward King and Emma S. Thorne, whose mother was Emily A. Vanderbilt, a daughter of Commodore Vanderbilt. They lived in England before purchasing large mining estates in Mexico, and established Guadalupe Ranch near Santa Barbara, California. After his death, she gave in his memory a Gilbert Stuart painting of George Washington to the Huntington Art Gallery in Pasadena. Louise King Baring was a cousin of JIC member William K. Vanderbilt. Her mother married as her second husband JIC member James Cresson Parrish.

DR. LEWELLYS FRANKLIN BARKER (1867 – 1943), physician. An internationally-known authority on eugenics, heredity, and neurology, Barker was a professor of medicine at Johns Hopkins University. He helped eliminate bubonic plague in the Philippines in 1899 and in San Francisco in 1901.

JOHN SANFORD BARNES (1835 – 1911), banker. He was a member of the banking firm headed by JIC member John S. Kennedy. Barnes served as president of the International Railroad Company of Texas and of the St. Paul & Pacific Railroad. He and his family lived in New York City and at "Coldbrooke" in Lenox, Massachusetts.

JOHN CONNOR BARRON (JIC member 1886-1899), physician. After serving in the battle at Bull Run, Barron was a practicing physician and a founder of the Union League Club. He was elected rear commodore of the Seawanhaka and Corinthian Yacht Clubs. His daughter, May, married in 1904 John Foster Archbold, son of John D. Archbold, who was president of the Standard Oil Company of New Jersey. John F. Archbold gave the hospital in Thomasville, Georgia, in memory of his father.

FRANCIS DWIGHT BARTOW (1881 – 1945), banker. A partner at J. P. Morgan & Company, he died at his winter home, Brewton Plantation, near Charleston, South Carolina.

WILLIAM GERRISH BEALE (1854 -1923), attorney. Beale was a Chicago lawyer who practiced with Robert Todd Lincoln, son of the president. He represented the Chicago firms of several JIC members and wrote the wills of Marshall Field and Joseph Medill. Under Medill's will, Beale held in trust the majority of stock of the Chicago Tribune, along with Medill's two daughters. He was a trustee of the Chicago Elevated Railway and married in 1904 in Florence, Italy, Elizabeth, daughter of Malcolm Caruthers of Chicago. A public school in Chicago is named for him.

ANSON MCCOOK BEARD (1874-1929). Beard was a son-in-law of JIC member James J. Hill, having married his daughter Ruth, who later married a son of JIC member Pierre Lorillard and was eventually a member in her own right. The Beards lived in

New York City and at Cedarhurst, Long Island. Their grandson is the well-known naturalist photographer Peter Beard who lived at Hog Ranch, adjacent to the home of Karen Blixen (the writer Isak Dinesen) near the Ngong Hills of east Africa.

FREDERICK WILDER BELLAMY (1887 – 1955), lawyer. He was senior partner in the Wall Street investment firm of Dominick & Dominick. Bellamy married in Brooklyn, New York, in 1914, Florence, daughter of John J. Walton, and they lived in New York City and in Katonah, New York.

SAMUEL READING BERTRON (1865 – 1938), banker. Originally from Mississippi, he was president of the international banking firm of Bertron, Griscom & Company of New York and Philadelphia. Bertron was active in the peace negotiations between Italy and Turkey in 1912 and received a Chevalier of the Crown of Italy in 1917. The Belgian government awarded him the King Albert Medal in the same year and he was also decorated by France and Romania.

LYNFORD BIDDLE (1876 – 1941), attorney. A Philadelphia lawyer who was well-known as an international cricket player, Biddle was unmarried and lived at "Lanoraie," the family home in Chestnut Hill in Philadelphia.

CORNELIUS KINGSLAND GARRISON BILLINGS (1861 – 1937), yachtsman and horse breeder. The Chicago fortune Billings inherited from his father was reported to be $80 million. In 1911 he became Chairman of the Board of Union Carbide. His large yacht, the *Vanadis* (mentioned by Edith Wharton in her diaries),

with him aboard, rammed the steamer *Bunker Hill* in 1915 and two people were killed. He rebuilt a later version by the same name and it now serves as a hotel in Sweden. Billings was also known as a breeder of champion horses at his Long Island estate, "Farnsworth." In New York City he bought Fort Tryon, the highest point on Manhattan, as a site for his horse stables, and for its opening he gave a white tie dinner party at which each guest sat on horseback throughout the evening. His lavish home at the site is now the Cloisters, housing the Metropolitan Museum of Art's medieval branch. He also kept a five thousand acre estate in Virginia, but late in life sold his eastern holdings and moved to Santa Barbara, California, where he died at Billings Park. His wife, Blanche, nursed him during his illness of bronchial pneumonia but contracted the disease from him and died ten days after his death. They were given a double burial service in Chicago and their daughter was the sole heir of their estates.

CLINTON LEDYARD BLAIR (1867 – 1949), banker and yachtsman. Blair and his brother, fellow JIC member John, were grandsons of John Insley Blair who founded Blairstown, New Jersey, and built the first four railroads west of Chicago. Their father was DeWitt Clinton Blair and their maternal uncle was Charles Scribner, founder of the publishing house. Ledyard, as he was called, joined the family's Wall Street banking firm, Blair & Company, and was a governor of the New York Stock Exchange as well as a railroad director. Blair was commodore of the New York Yacht Club, and his yacht, *Diana*, was turned over to the government for use in World War I. In 1914 he was aboard the German liner *Kronprinzessin Cecile* from New York City to Plymouth. As it approached Plymouth with $13.5 million in gold and silver aboard, it was advised to return to the U.S. because the outbreak of war had occurred during their journey. Because of the danger of a German ship's being captured by British ships in New York City, it was thought advisable not to dock there. With Blair's intimate sailing knowledge, he personally piloted the ship safely into Bar Harbor, Maine, where his family had a home, "Blair Eyerie." His first wife, Florence Osborne Jennings, by whom he had four daughters, died in 1931 and in 1936 he married Harriet Stewart Brown, widow of T. Suffern Tailer and daughter of Baltimore banker Alexander Brown (her brother, McEvers Bayard Brown, was a JIC member). They lived at "Blairsden," a Louis XIII-styled thirty-eight room mansion near Peapack, New Jersey (built at a cost of $2 million), and entertained at their Newport home, "Honeysuckle Lodge," as well as their Bermuda home, "Deepdene."

JOHN INSLEY BLAIR II (1876-1939), art collector. A brother of JIC member Clinton Ledyard Blair, their father's $60 million fortune was made in railroads and the banking firm of Blair & Company. Their grandfather, John Insley Blair, was president of sixteen railroads and owned more miles of railroad track than anyone alive at the time. John II was never active at the family firm but spent much of his career collecting art. He donated much of his collection of Americana as well as extensive visual art to the Museum of the City of New York as well as the Metropolitan Museum of Art.

C. K. G. Billing's 1903 white-tie dinner on horseback attended by liveried footmen.

Their father was chairman of the governing committee of Tuxedo Park and their sisters were the very social Mrs. Screven Lorillard and Mrs. Henry O. Havemayer, Jr.

JOHN AMORY LOWELL BLAKE (1879 – 1938), banker. Blake was a Boston banker and broker as a partner in Blake Brothers. He was an avid supporter of Harvard. After his first wife, Helen Prince, died, he married Anne Lindsay, who died in 1928. In 1930 he married Phyllis Tuck Cabot, widow of Norman W. Cabot, who was a football All-American at Harvard in 1896 and an airman in World War I.

GEORGE BLEISTEIN (1861 – 1918), publisher. Bleistein's parents were poor German immigrants who came to America in 1836. He dropped out of public school at the age of fourteen to support himself and went to work at the *Buffalo Courier*, where he eventually became president at the age of twenty-three. After the *Courier* was sold, he managed its large printing business and was executor of the estate of his mentor, Charles W. McCune. In 1886, he married McCune's daughter, Elizabeth, and they had two sons and one daughter. Bleistein was a director of the Pan American Exposition held at Buffalo in 1901 and is buried in Buffalo's Forest Lawn Cemetery. He was instrumental in founding the town of Cody, Wyoming, with several other Buffalo residents including JIC member Dexter Rumsey.

CORNELIUS NEWTON BLISS, SR. (1833 – 1911), financier and philanthropist. He was a partner and chairman of the board of Bliss, Fabyan & Company, a wholesale dry goods firm, where his partner was JIC member George Fabyan. In 1892, he became treasurer of the Republican National Committee. He served two

Top: George Bleistein, a son of German immigrants who became president of the Buffalo Courier at the age of twenty-three.

Bottom: George Bleistein, standing far left behind "Buffalo Bill" Cody, with fellow Jekyll member Dexter Rumsey, standing far right. This group is credited with having founded Cody, Wyoming.

years as secretary of the interior under President McKinley and was asked to accept the nomination of the vice presidency in 1900 but declined. Had he accepted, he would have become president when McKinley was assassinated in 1901. Bliss served as chairman of the board of the Metropolitan Opera and twice declined the nomination as governor of New York. In 1899 President McKinley, Vice President Hobart, and Speaker of the House Reed all visited Jekyll as guests of Bliss. His son, Neil, and daughter, Lizzie, were also JIC members.

CORNELIUS NEWTON BLISS, JR. (1874 – 1949), financier. "Neil" was a partner at Bliss, Fabyan, & Company and lived at Westbury, Long Island, where his sister commissioned Maurice Prendergast to paint a mural for the entrance hall. He was a Harvard graduate and succeeded his father as chairman of Bliss, Fabyan & Company until 1932. He also succeeded his father as treasurer of the Republican National Committee. In World War I he was a member of President Wilson's War Council and in World War II he was chairman of the Red Cross advisory council on war activities.

JEANNETTE ATWATER DWIGHT BLISS (Mrs. George Theodore Bliss) (JIC member 1919-1923). Her husband, a banker who founded and was the first commodore of the Erie Yacht Club, died in 1901. In 1908, Jeannette Bliss commissioned John LaFarge to design a stained glass window for the grand staircase of her home at 9 E. 68th Street in New York City. The allegory of Welcome—a classically garbed figure in the pose of Andromeda—draws back a portiere with her left hand and beckons the visitor

with her right. The model was the Bliss's daughter, Susan Dwight Bliss, who donated many La Farge watercolors to the Metropolitan Museum. The window is now in the American Wing of the Metropolitan Museum of Art. The daughter continued her father's book collection and donated it to Bowdoin College, where it is housed in the Susan Dwight Bliss Room, a baroque-style room with a sixteenth century ceiling taken from a Neapolitan palazzo. She also gave to Princeton Library a collection of one hundred and forty volumes published from the fifteenth through the twentieth centuries, many of them concerned with royal ceremonies and occasions involving royalty, in memory of her mother. Susan Dwight Bliss was a founding member of the social service executive board of St. Luke's Hospital and served for many years on the hospital's Auxiliary. Besides her work with St. Luke's, she was active in many other organizations concerned with the social and medical welfare of children and of psychiatric patients. She never married and died in 1966. She left her extensive collection of autographs and French manuscripts to Harvard, endowed a chair in epidemiology at Yale, and gave land for a nature center in New Canaan, Connecticut, on the site of her former arboretum. She was left $1.2 million by her mother, and was at one time supposedly engaged to a dubious "Count Soissons."

LIZZIE "LILLIE" PLUMMER BLISS (1864 - 1931), art collector and philanthropist. Lillie was the daughter of JIC member Cornelius Newton Bliss, Sr., and sister of JIC member Cornelius Bliss, Jr. Until she was fifty-nine in 1923, she cared for her invalid mother, whose spirit had been broken by the death of two young children. She also acted as hostess when her father entertained at large parties in Washington when he was U. S. secretary of the interior. Lillie was an arts protégé of JIC member Dr. Christian A. Herter, who taught her the intricacies of modern painting. In 1913 she supported the first Armory show introducing New York City to modern art by lending a Degas and a Renoir from her collection. She purchased her first Cezanne in 1916 and, at her death, she owned twenty-six of his works. In 1921 the Metropolitan Museum was convinced to mount its first Impressionist exhibition and Bliss loaned twelve paintings, including five Cezannes. The reaction was violently negative, but Bliss continued collecting and in 1926 purchased an important Gauguin that had been reviled by critics as "vile, Bolshevik" work. Her parents did not share her taste in art and her collection was relegated to the third floor of the family's townhouse, where Lillie commissioned Arthur B. Davies to paint a mural for the music room adjacent to her bedroom. After her mother's death she purchased a three-storey, 11,500 square-foot art moderne apartment on Park Avenue so that she could live among her collection. In 1929 Bliss met with four art enthusiasts at the home of Abby Aldrich Rockefeller, daughter of JIC member Nelson Aldrich (the group included Conger Goodyear, cousin of JIC members), to establish New York's Museum of Modern Art. Ill with cancer, Lillie bequeathed her entire collection, including works by Degas, Seurat, Picasso, Van Gogh, Matisse, Daumier, and Toulouse-Lautrec, to the Museum during its first year but stipulated that an endowment must be raised to support it (the final $100,000 was given by Nelson A. Rockefeller in his mother's honor). Her contribution became the core of the Museum's collection. In 1931 she toured the Toulouse-Lautrec exhibition at the Museum and died ten days later with her brother, Neil, and his daughter, Eliza, at her bedside. Two months after her death, the Museum held a memorial service and opened an exhibition of her collection, which was toured by more than 32,000 people. Intensely private (she ordered that all her papers be burned upon her death), Bliss never married and was described by a friend as "apparently the gentlest, and certainly the most modest of women; she was absolutely independent in her taste and courageous as to her method of doing things."

EGIL BOECKMANN (1881 - 1955), physician. Boeckmann and his parents were Norwegian immigrants. He was a doctor in St. Paul, Minnesota, and the son-in-law of JIC member James J. Hill, having married Hill's daughter, Rachel, in 1913. He was a founding director of the Minnesota Society for the Prevention of Blindness. Boeckmann and his wife were generous benefactors of the Minnesota Institute of Arts, donating paintings by Corot and Millet, which had been part of her father's extensive art collection.

FRANK STUART BOND (1830 – 1912), railroad president. Bond was a major and aide-de-camp at the Battle of Chickamauga. He lived in New London, Connecticut, and was a member of the Union Club. Bond was appointed president of the Philadelphia & Reading Railroad as well as vice president of the Chicago, Milwaukee & St. Paul Railway Company. He died, unmarried, at Jekyll Island in his eighty-third year.

MATTHEW CHALONER DURFEE BORDEN (1842 – 1912),

Left: Cornelius N. Bliss, Sr., Secretary of the Interior under President McKinley. Had he accepted McKinley's invitation to serve as Vice President, Bliss would have been President when McKinley was assassinated.

Bottom: Jekyll Island Club House in its early days.

Left: Frederick G. Bourne. Two of his daughters and three of his sons-in-law were also Jekyll members.

Above: Marion C. Bourne at the Mineola dog show with the best American-bred Russian wolfhound. She was a close friend of widowed Jekyll member William Rockefeller whose family feared they might marry.

manufacturer. Borden was the largest cotton manufacturer and printer in the world. In 1897, 1899, and 1901 he relieved a crisis in the industry by buying up vast quantities of cloth from his competitors when the market was overloaded. He also increased wages when others were laying off their employees. His yacht, the *Sovereign,* was purchased by the government and renamed the *Scorpion.* When his wife, Harriet, died in 1902, he closed all his factories for a full week. They lived in New York City and at "The Park" in Oceanic, New Jersey.

FREDERICK GILBERT BOURNE (1851 – 1919), financier and yachtsman. As a young man, Bourne was befriended by Alfred Corning Clark, who attended the church where Bourne sang in the choir. Clark, who had inherited the Singer Sewing Machine Company from his father, offered Bourne a position at Singer, where he eventually became president after his mentor's death. Bourne was commodore of the New York Yacht Club and built a castle on Dark Island in the St. Lawrence River. He became president of the Jekyll Island Club in 1914 and served until his death. His Long Island estate, "Oakdale," consisted of three thousand acres bordering that of JIC member William K. Vanderbilt. He gave $500,000 to the Cathedral of St. John the Divine for a choir school and installed a pipe organ at Oakdale. Two of his daughters, Marion and Marjorie, and three of his sons-in-law, Robert G. Elbert, Alexander D. Thayer, and Ralph B. Strassburger, were JIC members. In 1921 a stained glass window designed and signed by Louis Comfort Tiffany was dedicated in Bourne's memory at Jekyll's Faith Chapel. Its theme, "David Set Singers Before the Lord," was assumed to be a double allusion both to Bourne's musical talents as well as the name of the company he headed. A family struggle ensued over his $40 million estate, and his Long Island home, "Indian Neck Hall," was sold to a syndicate when his children could not agree to its disposition.

MARION C. BOURNE (Mrs. Robert George Elbert) (JIC member 1919-1937). A daughter of JIC member Frederick G. Bourne, she married JIC member Robert George Elbert. She was elected a member in her own right in 1919, one year before her sister, Marjorie. After her father's death, she took over his Jekyll apartment at Sans Souci. She became close to JIC member William Rockefeller during his widowhood and there was speculation they might marry.

MARJORIE BOURNE (Mrs. Alexander Dallas Thayer) (1888 – 1962). The youngest daughter of JIC member Frederick G. Bourne, her family called her "Hooley." She was elected a JIC member in her own right in 1920, one year after her sister. A wealthy young woman, she divided her time between homes in France and Pennsylvania as well as her father's extensive estate, "Dark Island Castle," on the St. Lawrence River. In 1923, while still unmarried, she purchased Fairbank Cottage at Jekyll from the Strassburgers. In 1926, attended by Countess Stephanie Beniezky, she married at her parents' Pennsylvania estate well-known athlete Alexander Dallas Thayer, who became a JIC member in 1929. The couple commissioned a new yacht, the *Queen Anne,* in 1931, and spent much of their time on board. They also had a home in Miami Beach. After Marjorie's death in 1962, Thayer married her sister,

Florence, who was divorced from her former husband, Anson Hard.

GEORGE STEPHENSON BREWSTER (JIC member from 1919; died 1936). He and his brother, JIC member Robert, were sons of Standard Oil partner Benjamin B. Brewster.

ROBERT STANTON BREWSTER (1875 - 1939), real estate developer. Brewster's father, Benjamin B. Brewster, went to California in the 1849 gold rush and became a mercantile partner of Oliver Burr Jennings. They retired several years later and returned east to become early and substantial partners of JIC member William Rockefeller, whose wife was a sister of Mrs. Jennings. Brewster's daughter, Mary, married Jennings' son, Oliver Gould Jennings (their New York City home is now the Lycee Francais de New York), and their son, Benjamin Brewster Jennings, was eventually president of Mobil Oil. Mary Brewster Jennings was the sister of JIC members Annie Burr Jennings, Emma Jennings Auchincloss, Walter Jennings, and Helen Jennings James. Robert Stanton Brewster was president of the Metropolitan Opera and Real Estate Company, which owned the Opera site and its building. He succeeded JIC member Robert Fulton Cutting as president of the Metropolitan Opera while fellow JIC member Cornelius Bliss was chairman of the board. Brewster's Delano-designed home "Avalon," was a massive estate in the manner of a French chateau in Mt. Kisco, New York. It burned in 1902. The merchant ship *S. S. Benjamin Brewster* burned two-and-a-half miles off the Grand Isle, Louisiana, shore after it was torpedoed by a German U-boat on July 9, 1942.

CALVIN STEWART BRICE (1845 – 1898), railroad president and U. S. Senator. Brice was president of the Lake Erie & Western Railroad and a director of many others. He unsuccessfully managed Grover Cleveland's re-election campaign for president in 1888 and in the next year he was chairman of the Democratic National Committee. In 1890 Brice was elected U.S. senator from Ohio. At his retirement from the Senate in 1897, he moved his family to New York City, where they became active in society. Brice was prominent in the development of Miami University in Ohio. At the time of his death, he was negotiating to build a railroad through China, where he had purchased exclusive rights across the country.

JACOB PERCY BRINTON (1863 -1948). He was a son of Frederick C. Brinton and Mary Huey Brinton of Delaware County, Pennsylvania. His cousin, Elizabeth Brinton, married John D. Drexel, cousin of JIC member Anthony Joseph Drexel Paul.

CHARLES STELLE BROWN (1851-1935). Brown married Lucy Nevins; their son was Congressman Lathrop Brown (1883-1959) from New York. After his wife's death, he married in 1924 (the same year he joined the JIC), Mary Jay Schieffelin, a great-granddaughter of William H. Vanderbilt. She was president of the Junior League of New York City, 1926-28.

MCEVERS BAYARD BROWN (1852- 1926), New York banker and yachtsman. He was a son of banker Alexander S. Brown and a grandson of Robert Bayard. His annual income was approximated at $1 million dollars. Having sold his first yacht, *Lady Torfrida,* to Grand Duke Michael of Russia, Brown purchased a one-thousand-ton replacement, originally built for Edward VII when Prince of Wales. Russia's Tsar Nichols II was negotiating to buy it when Brown upped his offer to $210,000. Named *Valfreyia*, the yacht became his home for the remainder of his life. Brown built the first cottage at Jekyll (where his Cutting cousins were also members) but never lived in it. At the age of thirty-seven, supposedly after a failed love affair, he sailed aboard his yacht and docked on the Colne River near Brightlingsea, England, eventually earning the name, "the millionaire hermit of the Essex coast." The yacht, fully outfitted, was always at ready with full provisions and crew. He kept bodyguards on board but no one else was allowed to sleep aboard the yacht. After reading his mail and American newspapers, Brown threw them all into the fire. Brown was known as a great philanthropist by the local residents, who often received gifts from him for little or no reason. During World War I his yacht was placed in dry dock with Brown still living on board. He never married and remained a Jekyll member until his death. His substantial fortune was left to his Cutting cousins, including the Marchesa Val d'Orca, the writer known as Iris Origo. In 1928 the *Valfreyia* was renamed the *Star of India* and fitted for cruising in Eastern waters under the ownership of the Maharajah of Nawanagar, better known as the cricketer "Ranji."

EDWARD LIVINGSTON BURRILL (JIC member 1927-1931; died 1937), broker. A member of the New York Stock Exchange, Burrill was a partner in the Wall Street firm of E. A. Pierce & Company. His granddaughter, Ellen Tuck French, married John J. Astor, whose father was lost on the *Titanic*. John J. Astor's mother was Madeleine Force Astor, who, as a widow, married JIC member William Karl Dick.

Top left: Kate Brice costumed as the Infanta Margarita (after Velazquez) at the Bradley Martin Ball of 1897. Her costume was designed by Worth in Paris and she had to be lowered into it the night of the Ball.

Top right: Her mother, Mrs. Calvin Brice, dressed for the same event. The New York Times described her "superb jewels" while the Sun marveled at her "glitter of gold and jewels." Her husband, who was to die the next year, was costumed as the Marquis de Lafayette.

Bottom: The Brice family at home in Ohio.

CORNELIA "NELLIE" STEWART SMITH BUTLER (Mrs. Prescott Hall Butler) (1846 – 1915). She was a daughter of J. Lawrence Smith of Smithtown, Long Island, and Sarah Nicoll Clinch Smith. Her sister, Bessie, was married to architect Stanford White; their brother, James Clinch Smith, witnessed the murder of White and died on the *Titanic.* Along with her sister, she inherited a substantial fortune from their aunt, Cornelia Clinch Stewart, wife of department store magnet A. T. Stewart. The Stewart funds allowed Bessie White to purchase the land in St. James that eventually became the Stanford Whites' home, "Box Hill." White met his future wife while working on designs for the Butler home. Nellie's family's heirs developed Garden City, New York, where many of the streets bear family names.

PRESCOTT HALL BUTLER (JIC member 1895-1901), attorney. As newlyweds, the Butlers lived in a Manhattan apartment next door to the young Charles McKim and his wife. They remained life-long friends and McKim eventually introduced his partner, Stanford White, to Mrs. Butler's sister, Bessie Smith. After White married Bessie Smith in 1884, they rented a house across the road from the Butlers. The Whites eventually purchased the site and he designed and furnished their home there, "Box Hill." Stanford White later designed the dining room of the Butlers' home, "Bytharbor," in St. James, New York. The house, designed by McKim and White at Nissequogue, is now on the National Register of Historic Places. As a favor to their uncle, Stanford White, the Butlers' sons, Lawrence Smith Butler, and Charles Stewart Butler, were sculpted as boys by Augustus Saint-Gauden in 1880-81. The work is now at the National Gallery of Art.

JAMES BYRNE (1857 – 1942), corporate lawyer. A prominent attorney in New York City, Byrne was chancellor of the board of regents of the State University of New York. The first Catholic elected to Harvard's seven-man governing body, he was instrumental in establishing Rice University in Houston. Byrne's daughter, Helen, married Hamilton Fish Armstrong whose father, Maitland Armstrong, designed the stained glass window in Jekyll's Faith Chapel. Their Long Island 353 acre estate, "Planting Fields," was sold in 1913 to W. R. Coe, the partner of JIC member Andrew F. Higgins. The site is now an arboretum encompassing 400 acres.

LEGRAND BOUTON CANNON (1815 - 1906), New York City banker and corporate director. Cannon served in the Union army and later wrote *Personal Reminiscences of the Rebellion, 1861-1866.* After his death, his widow married Theodore Frelinghuysen. Cannon's son, LeGrand, Jr., was a novelist who wrote *Look to the Mountain* and other historical novels. He and his wife died in a fire on their thousand-acre plantation on the banks of Black River near Georgetown, South Carolina.

AMORY SIBLEY CARHART (1898-1966), bank director. Carhart's father was a director of the Peoples Trust Company and an active clubman, while his grandfather was president of the National Bank of the Republic of New York as well as the Harlem Railroad Company. His family lived at "Villa Blanca" in Tuxedo Park. He also had a home in Northeast Harbor, Maine, as well as an estate in Warrenton, Virginia, where he was Master of the Hounds. The Carhart mansion at Fifth Avenue and 95th Street still stands

The entrance to "Planting Fields," the Byrne home in Long Island, which is now an arboretum.

"Bytharbor," the Saint James, Long Island home of Nellie and Prescott Butler, designed by noted architect Charles McKim who introduced them to his partner, Stanford White. White eventually married Nellie's sister and they built "Box Hill" near the Prescotts.

Top: Beatrice Claflin Breese, later Countess of Gosford.

Bottom: John Claflin, who was, at his death, the only surviving original member of the Jekyll Island Club.

and has been converted to four luxury condominiums. Carhart's father was a groomsman at the 1888 wedding of *Titanic* owner Bruce Ismay to Julia Florence Schieffelin.

ARTHUR OSGOOD CHOATE (1875 - 1962), investment broker and corporate director. Choate was a member of Potter, Choate and Prentice till the firm was dissolved when he became a senior partner in Clark, Dodge & Company. Choate's brother, William, founded the Choate School while their brother Joseph was the United States' ambassador to the Court of St. James. Choate's wife, Anne Hyde, was a god-daughter of Juliette Gordon Low, founder of the Girl Scouts, and succeeded her as the second president of that organization. Mrs. Choate was a survivor of the *Titanic,* along with her sister and brother, although their father perished. Anne Hyde Choate was instrumental in saving the Juliette Gordon Low birthplace in Savannah as a memorial to her godmother as well as the headquarters of the Girl Scouts. The Choates lived in Pleasantville, New York.

ARTHUR BRIGHAM CLAFLIN (1858 - 1939), wholesale dry goods merchant. Claflin was a partner in the firm founded by his father, Horace B. Claflin. His brother, John, was a JIC member. Claflin's estate on Long Island is now the campus of Southampton College; another of his estates is now Lakewood Country Club in New Jersey, whose first president was JIC member George Gould. Claflin's daughter, Beatrice, first married Robert P. Breese, son of James L. Breese, amateur photographer and close friend of architect Stanford White. Robert Breese's sisters married Lord Willoughby de Eresby (later Earl of Ancaster) and Lord Robert Innes-Ker, son of the

7th Duke of Roxburghe, while his first cousin May Parsons married the 4th Prince zu Lynar. In 1928 Beatrice Claflin Breese married the 5th Earl of Gosford.

JOHN CLAFLIN (1850 - 1938), mercantile merchant. Claflin, brother of JIC member Arthur, headed the United Dry Goods Company, capitalized at $51 million, and said to be the largest firm of its kind. His firm almost went bankrupt at the outbreak of the Civil War when it lost its southern market but he successfully guided it back to success. Claflin was a world explorer who financed and participated in dangerous expeditions throughout the world. At the time of his death at "Lindenwold," in Morristown, New Jersey, he was the only surviving original member of the JIC.

EDWARD WHITE CLARK (1828-1904), banker. Clark was the senior member of E. W. Clark & Company, Philadelphia bankers. He married Mary Todhunter Sill and lived in Germantown near Philadelphia. Of their children, Percy married Elizabeth Roberts, daughter of the president of the Pennsylvania Railroad, and Mary Todhunter "Tod" Clark married in 1930 Nelson Aldrich Rockefeller, governor of New York and U. S. vice president under Gerald Ford (as well as a grandson of JIC member Nelson Aldrich). She was the mother of his five children (one of whom was lost in Papua, New Guinea). Their divorce in 1962 was widely considered to have weakened his chances for winning the 1964 Republican presidential nomination. Edward W. Clark's grandson, Joseph S. Clark, II, was mayor of Philadelphia and United States senator from Pennsylvania.

HERBERT LINCOLN CLARK (1866 - 1940), broker. Clark was a governor of the Philadelphia Stock Exchange and partner at his family firm, E. W. Clark & Company. Along with his two brothers, he was among the best cricket players in the U.S. One of his daughters was married to Arthur B. Sinkler, president of the Hamilton Watch Company.

STEPHEN CARLTON CLARK (1882 - 1960), corporate director. He was a son of Alfred Corning Clark, founder of the Singer Sewing Machine Company, who chose JIC member Frederick G. Bourne to succeed him as president. After the senior Clark's death, his mother married the prominent and powerful Episcopal Bishop Henry C. Potter of New York. At the time wags said that he fell in love with the widow's mite and she fell in love with the bishop's mitre; within a month of their 1902 marriage, she contributed $500,000 to build East Side Community House. Stephen Clark served in France in World War I and was a director of the Singer Sewing Machine Company and New York Trust Company. He was chairman of the board of the New York State Historical Association, president of the Clark Foundation, director of the Scriven Foundation, and president of the National Baseball Hall of Fame at Cooperstown, New York, where his home, "Fernleigh," was located (he provided the funds to build the museum). Clark was chairman of the Museum of Modern Art from 1939 to 1946 and a trustee of the Metropolitan Museum of Art. He was publisher of the *Evening News* in Albany, New York, and the *Knickerbocker Press,* as well as a collector of Rembrandt, Van Gogh, Degas, Matisse, Renoir, Cezanne, Corot, and Picasso, most of which were donated to museums. His gifts to the Yale Museum included works by Copley, Eakins, Manet, Homer, Hopper, Picasso, and Van Gogh, and his will included $11.6 million in bequests. His

Conyers Manor, the Greenwich, Connecticut, home of Edmund C. Converse, sited on two thousand acres with a live-in staff of more than two hundred.

family foundations continue to provide considerable financial support to many causes.

THOMAS CURTIS CLARKE (1827 – 1901), civil engineer. Clarke, a Philadelphia native, specialized in bridge engineering and pioneered the modern iron viaduct. He built the first bridge across the Mississippi River at Quincy, Illinois, in fifteen months for the Burlington Railroad. In 1888 he built the Poughkeepsie Bridge across the Hudson and in 1890 built the Hawkesbury Bridge in Australia. Clarke served as president of the American Society of Civil Engineers. He joined the Union Bridge Company where his partners included JIC members George S. Field, Edmund Hayes, Thomas C. Clarke, and Charles S. Maurice.

ROBERT CHARLES CLOWRY (1838 – 1925), telegraph company president. Clowry was in charge of union military telegraph operations during the Civil War. He eventually became president and general manager of Western Union Telegraph Company and its subsidiaries. He and his wife, Caroline Eastabrook, lived in Tarrytown, New York.

ALEXANDER COCHRANE (1840- 1919), chemical manufacturer. Cochrane was president of the Cochrane Chemical Company of Boston, whose technical advisor was Alexander Graham Bell. Through Bell, Cochrane became one of the original directors and earliest stockholders of American Bell Telephone Company and a director in many railroad companies and banks. Among his children was Ethel, an artist known as Lily, who married artist Howard Gardner Cushing. After his death she married in 1925 JIC member James D. Sawyer. Her son, Alexander Cochrane

Cushing, founded Squaw Valley and successfully located the 1960 winter Olympics there. Her granddaughter, Lily Dulany Emmet, married Anthony West, son of H. G. Wells and Rebecca West. The Cushings' daughter, Alexandra, is married to historian and author Arthur Schlesinger, Jr.

HENRY EDWARD COE (1895 - 1954), broker. Coe was a Navy officer who served in World War II before entering the stock brokerage business. He was a member of the New York Stock Exchange and a director of the New York Philharmonic Symphony. His wife, Eunice James, was a daughter of JIC member Walter James.

LAWRENCE M. CONDON (1899 – 1973). Condon was a Columbia graduate and resident of Southampton, New York. In June 1941 he wrote his *Survey of the Relationship of Columbia College to Columbia University,* presented to the university as his class's twentieth anniversary gift. "Funds and assets originally intended for the purposes of Columbia College," the Survey contended, "have been employed ... [to build] a huge, many-sided University." As for Columbia College, Condon continued, "It seems fair to say that its best interests have not been served but have in fact been subordinated."

EDMUND COGSWELL CONVERSE (1849 - 1921), inventor and banker. Converse invented a tube coupler widely in use in manufacturing. In 1899 he merged twenty iron and steel tube companies into the National Tube Company, capitalized at $80 million, retired in 1901, and entered banking. He became President of Bankers Trust Company and Liberty National Bank in New

York City. Among his protégés, known as "Converse boys," were JIC member Henry P. Davison and Benjamin Strong, Converse's son-in-law. His home in Greenwich was the two-thousand-acre Conyers Manor with forty buildings and a live-in staff of over two hundred. In 1915 he gave the Converse Library to Amherst College. He wintered in Pasadena, California, where he died, and his will was probated at $31 million. Among his children was Antoinette, Baroness Von Romberg (formerly Mrs. Walter C. Morrill), whose husband, Baron Maximilian von Romberg, served as a captain in the 80th Prussian Fusiliers and was killed in action on 22 Sept 1914 seven years after their marriage. Antoinette's sister, Katherine Peabody Converse, married Benjamin Strong, Jr., president of Bankers Trust Company of New York, who was elected the first governor of the Federal Reserve Bank of New York at the Bank's first board meeting in 1914. He was still in that post at his death in 1928.

GEORGE COPPELL (JIC member 1900 – 1901; died 1901), banker. A native of Liverpool, England, in 1857 Coppell went to New Orleans as acting British Consul. In 1865 he moved to New York City and became a member of the banking firm of Maitland, Phelps & Company which became Maitland, Coppell & Company. His son, Arthur, became senior partner in the firm and died in 1934.

ERASTUS CORNING, JR. (1827 – 1897), iron manufacturer. Corning succeeded his father (1794-1872) as head of his family's merchant and railroad interests. In 1875 his father consolidated extensive iron mills in Albany, Hudson, and Fort Edward into one company (the plates and bars for the Confederacy's ironclad *Monitor* were manufactured by Corning's mills). The father also formed the largest U. S. corporation at the time, the New York Central, and controlled it until purchased by Cornelius Vanderbilt. In 1881, Erastus Corning, Jr., declined the Democratic Party's nomination for governor of New York (it was accepted by Grover Cleveland). His sons, Parker and Edward, were the driving force behind Albany's Democratic Party machine (Edwin served as New York's lieutenant governor and Parker was a U. S. congressman) and his grandson, Erastus II, was mayor of Albany for more than forty years. Erastus, Jr. was an orchid grower and butterfly collector.

ROBERT BAYARD COYKENDALL (1878 – 1913), railroad director. His father, Samuel D. Coykendall, was president of the Ulster and Delaware Railroad. His maternal grandfather, Thomas Cornell, established shipping lines on the Hudson River and made the towns of Kingston and Newburgh shipping ports. In 1902 Robert married Katharine Sahler, who was a cousin of Mrs. Edwin Gould.

CHARLES RICHARD CRANE (1858 - 1939), manufacturer and diplomat. Charles' father was Richard Teller Crane, Sr. (1832 -1912), a self-made Chicago manufacturer of bathroom fixtures, founder of the Crane Company and the Crane Elevator Company (sold to Otis Elevator Company in 1898). He and his family lived at "Jerseyhurst" on Geneva Lake. The father opposed university education and donated money for vocational training, which he thought preferable to a liberal arts education. He wrote an article decrying university education in which he claimed, "ninety percent of the students at Harvard University drink in their freshman year, ninety-five percent drink in their senior year, and fifteen percent go irretrievably to the bad." Crane was married twice and his son was a Yale graduate. The son succeeded his father as president of the family companies but in 1914, he sold his fifty percent share to his younger brother, JIC member Richard Teller Crane, Jr. Charles R. Crane fluently spoke French, German, Russian, Arabic, and Chinese. He was one of two American commissioners on mandates to Turkey in 1919 and his King-Crane Commission was largely responsible for beginning the import of oil from the Middle East. President Taft appointed him minister to China but before leaving the U.S. to accept the post, he was recalled because of a speech he made to which the Japanese objected. Crane switched his allegiance to the Democratic Party and President Wilson rewarded him with the post he had been denied, where he served from 1920 –21 (the post was later raised to ambassadorial rank). Crane was intimately involved in the creation of Czechoslovakia, having become close friends with Jan Masaryk when Crane endowed a chair at the University of Chicago that Masaryk filled. His son, Richard II, was private secretary to U.S. Secretary of State Lansing and later first minister to Czechoslovakia before becoming ambassador to China 1920-22. Crane was a large financial contributor to the Marine laboratory at Woods Hole, where he had a summer home. His daughter, Frances, married Tomas Masaryk, son of Czechoslovakia's founder. His son, John, accompanied his father

Interior stair hall of St. Petersburg's Beloselsky-Belozersky Palace, the home of Florence Crane's husband, Prince Serge.

on 1921 trips through Siberia and Russia and served as research and press secretary to the founding president of Czechoslovakia. In 1930 John was named head of the Institute of Current World Affairs which was financed by his father with an endowment. John married Countess Teresa Martini Marescotti (1909-1973).

FLORENCE HIGINBOTHAM CRANE (Mrs. Richard Teller Crane, Jr.) (1870 - 1949), philanthropist. Florence was a daughter of Harlow N. Higinbotham (1838-1919), designated by his partner, JIC member Marshall Field, to be president of The Chicago World's Fair and Columbian Exhibition of 1893. He was later president of The Field Museum for many years. Higinbotham was the original owner of a large area of land near Joliet known as the Pilcher parcel. In 1925 the heirs of Harlow N. Higinbotham donated 239 acres immediately east of Pilcher Park, named Higinbotham Woods, as a bird sanctuary and conservatory. Mrs. Crane was an active member of The Antiquarian Society of The Art Institute of Chicago and the contributor of its Crane Rooms. She arranged for a posthumous memorial to her husband known as the Crane Altar, designed by David Adler (who designed the Cranes' home at Jekyll), containing a copy of a Byzantine mosaic portrait of St. John Chrysostom, from the Hagia Sophia in Istanbul, in St. Chrysostom's Church, Chicago. She also commissioned the mausoleum for the Crane Family at Chicago's Graceland Cemetery and the monument for her brother and his descendants there as well. Mrs. Crane became a JIC member in her own right in 1919 even though her husband held his own membership until his death in 1931. Her sister, Alice, married Joseph Medill Patterson, editor and publisher of the Chicago Tribune and New York Daily News.

RICHARD TELLER CRANE, JR. (1873- 1931), manufacturer. The youngest son of Richard Teller Crane and Josephine Prentice, from 1914 he was president of his family's manufacturing company until his death. The company enjoyed its greatest success during his leadership, expanding to 20,000 employees and facilities in two hundred showrooms around the world. He first convinced the public that bathroom facilities should be as attractive as they are efficient. During his lifetime he distributed $12 million of his company's stock to his staff and his will left additional stock to long-time employees who had never sold his original gift. Crane married in 1904 Florence, daughter of Harlow Niles Higinbotham of Chicago, a partner of JIC member Marshall Field. Their children were Cornelius and Florence. During his lifetime Crane was reportedly the second-wealthiest man in Chicago after the founder of Sears, Roebuck. In 1917 the Cranes built their elaborate cottage at Jekyll, designed by David Adler, who later designed their palatial mansion, "Castle Hill," in Ipswich, Massachusetts. It was to be the largest and most expensive home built on the Island, boasting forty rooms, including seventeen baths – all, of course, outfitted with Crane fixtures. The fact that the Cranes' butler dressed in plum livery at Jekyll was not lost on the other members who prized the island's "simplicity." The Cranes' daughter, Florence, married Prince Serge S. Beloselsky-Belozersky, whose father had been aide-de-camp to the late Tsar Nicholas II. Prince Serge's mother was American heiress Susan Whittier whose father, General Charles Whittier, died on the *S.S. Mauretania* in the Atlantic in 1908.

FRANKLIN MUZZY CROSBY (1875 - 1947), food manufacturer. Crosby was vice president of General Mills, which

The Administration Building of Chicago's 1893 Columbia Exposition and World's Fair, chaired by Harlow Higinbotham, partner of Marshall Field and father of Jekyll member Florence H. Crane. Her sister, Alice, married Joseph M. Patterson, editor and publisher of **The Chicago** *Tribune* and New York Daily News.

The marriage of Countess Teresa Martini Marescotti and John Crane, son of Charles R. Crane.

Westbrook, the home of W. Bayard Cutting, landscaped by Frederick Law Olmsted

The W. Bayard Cutting family at Westbrook. The Cuttings' granddaughter, the Marchesa of Val d'Orcia, became known as the writer Iris Origo.

was founded by his father as the Washburn-Crosby Company, makers of Gold Medal Flour. He and his family lived at "Ferndale" outside Minneapolis.

ELLIOT CROSS (1884 -1949), architect. His Princeton real estate syndicate developed Sutton Place in New York City. During World War I, his wife, Martha, directed the Red Cross training of three thousand women working in canteens in France, and in World War II, she lobbied for establishment of the Women's Army Corps. Their son, James Elliot Cross, married a daughter of JIC member Robert Goelet IV and granddaughter of JIC member Ogden Goelet.

HERBERT EDWIN CROUCH (JIC member 1915-1921). A Buffalo native, he was a son of Herbert G. and Anna Lillian Crouch. His sister, Lillian, married Stephen Austin Watrous.

BRIGGS SWIFT CUNNINGHAM (1839 -1912), banker. Cunningham was a Cincinnati meat packer and banker, and a director of the Pennsylvania Railroad. He was president of the Citizens National Bank of Cincinnati, an early investor in Procter & Gamble, and donated Cunningham Hall to the University of Cincinnati. His son, Briggs, Jr., in 1930 married Lucie Bedford, granddaughter of a co-founder of Standard Oil. On his honeymoon he saw his first motor race at Monaco and, upon his return, created the Automobile Racing Club of America. In 1952 he placed fourth overall at LeMans and, in 1958, he skippered the American twelve-meter yacht, *Columbia,* to win the America's Cup. After his retirement, he built the Briggs Cunningham Automotive Museum in California to house all his racing cars. Known as the creator of

the first American sports car, at his death in 2003 he was inducted into the Motorsports International Hall of Fame. The America's Cup Hall of Fame had inducted him in 1993. His daughter was the wife of Stewart McKinney who represented Connecticut in the U. S. Congress for more than seventeen years.

ROBERT FULTON CUTTING (1852 -1934), financier. A brother of JIC member William Bayard Cutting, they were sons of Fulton and Justine Bayard Cutting. In the 1890s he was known as "the First Citizen of New York" because of his civic commitments and philanthropies as well as his fight against Tammany Hall and Republican bosses. In 1912 at his brother's death, he succeeded as president of their family businesses. Cutting was president of the Cooper Union, an early promoter of Tuxedo Park, and was decorated with the Belgian Order of Leopold II. His first wife, Natalie Schenck, died in 1875 leaving a son, R. Bayard. In 1883 he married Helen Suydam and had one son and three daughters, including Mrs. Reginald Auchincloss.

WILLIAM BAYARD CUTTING (1850 - 1912), attorney and railroad president. Brother of JIC member Robert Fulton Cutting, they were descendants of the Livingstons and Bayards of early New York Society. Cutting and his brother, Fulton, started the sugar beet industry in the U.S. in 1888. He was a builder of railroads, operated the ferries of New York City, and developed a part of the south Brooklyn waterfront. Cutting was president of the Union League Club and in 1887 hired Frederick Law Olmsted to landscape "Westbrook," a one thousand acre river estate with its now-famous Bayard Cutting Arboretum. He died on a special train of the Rock

Island Railroad conveying him east just as he was crossing the Mississippi River. He had been visiting his ill son, Bronson M. Cutting, in the mountains above Santa Fe, New Mexico, against his doctor's orders. The body of another son, W. Bayard, Jr., who had died two years previously in Egypt, was brought back to the U.S. and the two bodies were buried at the same time. His son, Bronson, was an advocate for the Hispanic natives of the southwest and published a Spanish language newspaper in New Mexico. He served in the U. S. Senate from 1927 until his death, unmarried, in an airplane accident in 1935. Mrs. Cutting died at Oakdale in 1949.

CHARLES WILLIAM DABNEY (1855 - 1945), university president. Dabney's father was chief of staff to General Stonewall Jackson. After earning a Ph.D., the son began his teaching career at Emory University, then at the University of North Carolina. From 1887 until 1904 he was president of the University of Tennessee. He was then appointed president of the University of Cincinnati and served in that capacity until 1920. He died at Asheville, North Carolina, while traveling from Florida to Cincinnati for his ninetieth birthday celebration. One daughter, Mrs. Alexander Thomson, was president of Western College in Oxford, Ohio, while another daughter, Mrs. John W. Ingle, served as dean of women at the University of Cincinnati. His two-volume work, *Universal Education in the South,* was published in 1936.

RICHARD HENRY DANA (1851 - 1931), author, attorney and civil service reformer. Six unbroken generations of his family graduated from Harvard, beginning with Richard Dana in 1718. His father was the author of *Two Years Before the Mast.* Dana was

an internationally-known expert on tax law, president of the board of the New England Conservatory of Music as well as the Boston YMCA. In 1878, he married Edith Longfellow, daughter of Henry Wadsworth Longfellow. Among their six children was Richard H., Jr., a New York City architect.

CHARLES MELDRUM DANIELS (1885 – 1973), "the greatest swimmer in the world." Daniels was an American swimmer who won seven Olympic medals and was the originator of the "American crawl," which became the predominant freestyle form. At the 1904 Olympic Games in St. Louis, Missouri, he was America's star swimmer, winning gold medals in the 220-yard and 440-yard freestyle and the 450-yard freestyle relay, as well as an additional silver medal. He married Florence Goodyear Wagner, sister of JIC member Frank H. Goodyear.

JOHN TILDEN DAVIS (born 1868; JIC member 1922-26). A native of St. Louis, he was the elder brother of Dwight Filley Davis (1879-1945), U.S. Secretary of War 1925-29, and Governor of the Philippine Islands 1929-32, who conceived the idea of an international tennis championship and convinced their father to donate the Davis Cup that bears his name. Their maternal grandfather, Oliver Dwight Filley, was mayor of St. Louis during the Civil War. JIC member Bernon Prentice was an early chairman of the Davis Cup Committee.

HENRY POMEROY DAVISON (1867 - 1922), financier. Davison was a partner at J. P. Morgan & Company and Chairman of the Executive Committee of Bankers Trust Company. Having served as president of the American Red Cross, in 1919 in Paris he

Henry P. Davison, protégé of Jekyll member Edmund C. Converse, marches in a New York City parade (note his initials inside the hat).

was elected chairman of the board of the World League of Red Cross Societies. He was a protégé of JIC member Edmund C. Converse and lived at "Peacock Point" in Locust Valley, New York. Among his children was F. Trubee, who married a daughter of Dr. Endicott Peabody, rector of Groton School.

CHARLES DEERING (1852 - 1927), manufacturer. Deering's father was the founder of Deering Milliken & Company. As a young Naval Academy graduate he was chosen by President and Mrs. Ulysses S. Grant to serve as their personal escort during their 1879 tour of China and Japan. He served as secretary of the Deering Harvester Company until its 1902 merger with International Harvester, when he became chairman of the board. An artist, Deering was a friend and student of John Singer Sargent. He purchased a ruined castle near Tarragona, Spain, which he called "Marycel," filled it with such Spanish masters as El Greco, and attempted to found an artist colony there. In 1910 his contribution to the Art Institute of Chicago enabled the acquisition of El Greco's *Assumption of the Virgin*. In 1924 he gave his extensive art collection to his two daughters and they continued his patronage of the Art Institute of Chicago as well as several other institutions. Deering died at his winter home in Miami not far from his brother James' estate, "Vizcaya." His will left half a million dollars to Northwestern University and his family matched that amount to found the Charles Deering Library. Substantial bequests also went to hospitals in Chicago and Miami. His son, Roger Deering, left over $7 million in an unrestricted gift to Northwestern University upon his death in 1936. A daughter, Marion, wed Chauncey McCormick, a grandson of William McCormick, founder of the farm machinery company, and a cousin of Colonel Robert McCormick, editor and publisher of the *Chicago Tribune*. (Chauncey McCormick's grandfather was JIC member Joseph Medill.)

ROBERT WEEKS DE FOREST (1848 - 1931), attorney and philanthropist. A partner with his brother, Henry, in the law firm of de Forest Brothers, he was general counsel for fifty years and vice president for twenty-two years of the Central Railroad of New Jersey. De Forest served as counsel for his close friend and fellow JIC member John S. Kennedy and helped implement his donation of the United Charities Building in New York City. In 1897, he incorporated the American Academy in Rome, and, in 1905 at the request of steel industrialist Henry Phipps, de Forest incorporated Phipps' $1 million donation to build affordable housing in the city, an endeavor that continues in today's Phipps Housing complex in Manhattan. De Forest was head of the Russell Sage Foundation and president of the Metropolitan Museum of Art, to which he gave his valuable collection of American furniture in 1924 (his father-in-law was the first president of the museum). His estate was at Cold Spring Harbor, Long Island, and one of his daughters married JIC member William A. W. Stewart.

JOHN DEKOVEN (1833 - 1898), banker. DeKoven was founder of the Northern Trust Company in Chicago. He married Helen Haddock who was born within the stockade of Fort Dearborn in Michigan. Their daughter, suffragist Louise deKoven Bowen, was president of the Women's Club of Chicago, a close associate of Jane Addams with whom she lived for many years, and became president

Top: Robert W. de Forest, president the Metropolitan Museum of Art to which he gave his valuable collectio of American furniture in 1924.

Bottom: Oheka, overlooking Cold Spring Harbor in Long Island, was the second-largest home in Americ (Biltmore was the first) and was designed by William A. Delano for Otto Kahn.

and trustee of Hull-House. She gave more than half a million dollars in her lifetime to women and children's organizations and, after her husband's death in 1911, donated seventy-two acres of land in Waukegan, Illinois, as a summer retreat for children of the Hull-House neighborhood. The DeKoven's grandson, John DeKoven Hill, was an apprentice of Frank Lloyd Wright and served as his primary interior designer. In 1945 Hill drew many of the plans for Wright's Lowell Walter residence in Quaueton, Iowa, and later served as chairman of the board of directors of the Frank Lloyd Wright Foundation.

EUGENE DELANO (1844 - 1920), banker. Delano was a senior member of the firm of Brown Brothers & Company. He was made a partner in Philadelphia in 1894 and moved to New York City where his brother-in-law, John Crosby Brown (they were married to sisters), a grandson of the founder of Brown Brothers, was then the senior member of the firm. Delano's father-in-law, Dr. William Adams, was for seven years president of the faculty of Union Theological Seminary. Delano was a trustee of Williams College, a member of Philadelphia's Rittenhouse Club, as well as the Penn Club. He was a member of the welcoming committee for the Imperial Japanese Mission to New York City in 1917. One of his sons, William Adams Delano, was a prominent artist and architect whose firm, Delano and Aldrich, was well known as designers of society country houses. His clients included Astors, Rockefellers, Vanderbilts, and Whitneys, but his first major commission was from JIC member Henry Walters to build an art museum in Baltimore to house his own collection. Delano designed the

second-largest residence (after the Biltmore estate) in the United States, "Oheka," overlooking Cold Spring Harbor on Long Island for financier Otto Kahn. Built in 1921 in French chateau style, with gardens by Frederick Law Olmsted, "Oheka" encompassed more than 109,000 square feet and was staffed with 125 people.

JOSEPHINE MOORE DEXTER (Mrs. Wirt Dexter) (JIC member 1896 – 1901). She was a teacher from Springfield, Massachusetts, who married in 1866 as his second wife JIC member Wirt Dexter. After her husband's death in 1890, she purchased a home in Boston's Back Bay and moved her family there. Her daughter, suffragist and philanthropist Katharine, married Stanley McCormick, son of Cyrus and brother of JIC member Cyrus, Jr.

SAMUEL DEXTER (JIC member from 1893 until his death in 1894). The original Samuel Dexter (1761-1816) was a Boston attorney who was secretary of war under President John Adams and secretary of the treasury under Presidents Adams and Jefferson. He was a United States senator from Massachusetts and refused the appointment as Minister to Spain. His son, Samuel, was a co-founder of the University of Michigan. The younger Samuel's son was JIC member Wirt Dexter.

WIRT DEXTER (1832 - 1890), attorney. Dexter was a lumberman in Michigan before moving to Chicago in 1853. He became a prominent attorney and a director of the Chicago, Burlington & Quincy Railroad. Dexter chaired the executive committee formed to distribute aid in the aftermath of the 1871 Chicago fire and gave up all business interests at the time to spend one year restoring order and distributing aid. The Wirt Dexter

Left: Mrs. Stanley McCormick (Katharine Dexter) and friend campaigning for women's suffrage, 1913. Her inheritance of thirty-five to forty million dollars enabled her to become a great philanthropist.

Right: Madeleine Force Astor Dick who survived the sinking of the Titanic as the pregnant young bride of John J. Astor IV. She later gave birth to his son but relinquished her claims to the substantial Astor estate to marry Jekyll member William K. Dick.

Building in Chicago was built in 1887. His clients included JIC member Marshall Field and George Pullman, who was elected to membership but declined. Dexter married in 1858 Kate Dusenberry, who died in 1864, and two years later he married Josephine Moore. Dexter chaired the committee that chose the architect to build the Jekyll Island Club's main building. His first cousin was JIC member Gordon McKay. Dexter's daughter, Katharine, married Stanley McCormick, youngest son of Cyrus and brother of JIC member Cyrus McCormick, Jr. Stanley suffered from schizophrenia and was hospitalized for decades; at his eventual death in 1947, she inherited $35-40 million and became a great philanthropist. She was an early advocate for birth control, a suffragist, a supporter of Margaret Sanger, and a major donor to Massachusetts Institute of Technology, where she received a degree in biology in 1904. She built their first women's dormitory and left an additional $25 million bequest to MIT.

JOHN HENRY DICK (1851- 1925), capitalist. Dick's father was one of the founders of Manufacturers Bank of Brooklyn. The son became a leader in sugar production as an officer in American Sugar Refining Company and National Refining Company. He was a partner with Cord Meyer in developing Long Island and was a large stockholder in St. Regis Paper Company. Dick died at his home, "Allen Winden," in Islip, Long Island. His daughter, Julia, married Kingsland Macy, son of JIC member George H. Macy. His son, William K. Dick, was also a JIC member.

WILLIAM KARL DICK (1888 - 1953), sugar manufacturer. A son of JIC member John Henry Dick, he was chairman of the board of National Sugar Refining Company. He married in 1916 Mrs. Madeleine Force Astor, widow of John Jacob Astor, who died on the *Titanic*. She gave up the Astor trust fund and mansions to marry, but divorced him in Reno in 1933. Dick then married Virginia Keniston Conner, a prominent interior designer who also designed furniture for Frank Lloyd Wright. Madeleine Astor Dick married Enzo Fiermonte, Italian middleweight boxer, whom she divorced in 1938 before dying in 1940 at her home in Palm Beach at the age of forty-seven. One of the Dick sons by Madeleine, John Henry Dick, was an ornithologist, painter, and illustrator who lived at Dixie Plantation near Charleston, South Carolina. At his death in 1995 he left his collection of rare books and Audubon prints, as well as his plantation, to the College of Charleston.

WATSON BRADLEY DICKERMAN (1846-1923), broker. Dickerman was president of the New York Stock Exchange and a partner in the brokerage firm of Dominick & Dickerman. He was president of the New York Zoological Society and bred thoroughbred horses at his estate at Mamoroneck, New York.

JOHN WESLEY DOANE (JIC member 1887-1896), wholesaler and banker. He was the founder of J. W. Doane & Co. of Chicago, importers and wholesalers of teas and coffees, and later president of Merchants' Loan and Trust Company of Chicago. Doane was a major investor in the Pullman Car Company and was president of Chicago's Commercial Club in 1879 and 1880, following its first president, Levi Leiter, co-founder of Marshall Field Company. He and his family lived on Prairie Avenue in Chicago one block away from JIC member Marshall Field and had a summer home in Thompson, Connecticut. The family of his daughter, Lily Doane Wicks, became a substantial donor to the University of Utah's art collection. His grandson, Bartlett Wicks, was U. S. consul for the principality of Monaco.

TRACY DOWS (1871 - 1937), landowner. Dows owned Fox Hollow Farm near Rhinebeck, New York, consisting of seven hundred acres. He was an 1893 graduate of Harvard and died in London, where he had lived for six months. In 1903 he married Alice Olin, a daughter of attorney Stephen H. Olin, whose wife was Emeline Dodge Harriman, a daughter of Oliver Harriman. Dows' elder sister, Susan, was married to JIC member Christian A. Herter. His son, Olin Dows, was a prominent artist who accompanied U. S. troops into battle in World War II and documented their heroics both in photographs and paintings. Dows' father was David Dows, for whom the grandest cargo schooner ever to sail the Great Lakes was named. It was, at the time, the largest five-masted schooner in the world but now lies on the bottom of Lake Michigan, a favorite destination for divers.

JOHN EUGENE DU BIGNON (1849-1930), developer. Owner of the Oglethorpe Hotel in Brunswick, Georgia, du Bignon was the local impetus for founding the Jekyll Island Club. The Island had been purchased in 1792 by the Sapelo Company comprised of four French landowners, among them Christophe Poulain du Bignon, John's grandfather. He and his descendants were the principal owners of the island until 1886. John Eugene du Bignon and his brother-in-law Newton Finney (married to du Bignon's sister) were the early developers of the Jekyll Island Club.

Between 1879 and 1885 the two men re-acquired Jekyll with the idea of forming a hunting club for wealthy northerners. In 1886 Finney, as a representative of the newly formed Jekyll Island Club, purchased the island from the du Bignons for $125,000. John du Bignon's house, constructed in 1884, still stands at Jekyll, although it was moved from its former location where Sans Souci now stands. (For more information on the du Bignon period of Jekyll Island, see June Hall McCash's book, *Jekyll Island's Early Years*, University of Georgia Press, 2005)

STUART DUNCAN (1872 - 1957), manufacturer. Duncan was chairman of the board of Lea & Perrins, manufacturers of sauces. He had been senior partner in John Duncan & Son, founded in 1819, which was dissolved in 1930 when it took over Lea & Perrins. In 1912 he built a palatial residence at Newport called "Bonniecrest," overlooking the Newport Harbor and designed by John Russell Pope, designer of the Jefferson Memorial in Washington. His wife was a sister of Mrs. William M. V. Hoffman, whose husband was a JIC member.

WILLIAM BRADFORD D'WOLF (JIC member 1886-1891), broker. D'Wolf was a partner in the New York stock brokerage firm of D'Wolf and Parsons. He was a member of the Union Club and a brother-in-law of JIC member Lloyd Aspinwall.

EDWARD EVERETT EAMES (1829 – 1906), merchant. Eames was a partner & vice president in the New York City merchant firm H. B. Claflin & Company owned by his cousins, JIC members John and Arthur Claflin. In the cotton goods market he was said to be the largest buyer in the world. His three sons all joined him in the firm.

(ALFRED) LEWIS EDWARDS (1836 - 1910), attorney. An 1857 member of Yale's Skull and Bones, he graduated from Harvard law school in 1861. Edwards practiced in New York City until retiring in old age to Athol, New York. An accomplished musician, he married in 1874 Arabella, daughter of Duncan Magee of Watkins, New York. Their daughter was Mrs. Archibald K. Mackay.

ROBERT GEORGE ELBERT (JIC member 1926-29), author. Elbert was the husband of Marion C. Bourne, daughter of JIC member Frederick C. Bourne, who became a member in her own right in 1919. In 1934, he wrote *Unemployment and Relief*, and in 1936, *An Answer to the Townsend Plan.*

HOWARD ELLIOTT (1860 - 1928), railroad president. Elliott was president of the New York, New Haven & Hartford Railroad, president of the Northern Pacific Railroads, and a director of many others. He was best known for averting the looming financial crisis of the New Haven Railroad and for implementing its successful rehabilitation. From 1903 until 1913 he lived with his family in St. Paul, Minnesota, where he was president of the Northern Pacific Railroads. In 1917, under threat of a nervous breakdown and on the advice of doctors, he resigned and continued only in an advisory capacity. Elliott served as an overseer of Harvard and a director of many corporations. He and his wife, Janet, were traveling by train in 1925 from Jekyll Island to their home in New York City when she became so ill that they broke their journey at Baltimore. She died there of pneumonia. One of their daughters, Edith, was married to JIC member Edmund P. Rogers. She died in childbirth at home

Mrs. Howard Elliott died en route from Jekyll Island to her New York City home.

during the birth of their second son in 1919. Rogers married in 1931 Dorothy Knox Goodyear, widow of JIC member Frank Henry Goodyear, Jr., who was killed in an auto accident.

RUDOLPH ELLIS (1837- 1915), banker. Ellis was president of the Fidelity Trust Company of Philadelphia, a director of the Pennsylvania Railroad Company and of American Telephone & Telegraph Company. His wife was Helen Struthers, whose brother, William, Ellis nominated for membership in the Club. William Struthers eventually built Moss Cottage at Jekyll. His daughter, Jean Struthers, married JIC member Henry Francis Sears with artist Mary Cassatt present at the wedding.

DUNCAN STEUART ELLSWORTH (JIC member 1895- 1908), coal supplier. Ellsworth was a partner in the family firm of Magee & Ellsworth founded by his father, Samuel Ellsworth, and maternal grandfather, John Magee. His family owned the Fall Brook Coal and Fall Brook Railway in Pennsylvania. He was a member of the Okatee Hunting Club in South Carolina and his son, Duncan, Jr., was known for organizing wildlife expeditions.

JAMES WILLIAM ELLSWORTH (1849 - 1925), coal supplier and philanthropist. He was president of James W. Ellsworth & Company of Cleveland, coal operators, until his retirement in 1900. Ellsworth revitalized his birth town of Hudson, Ohio, and matched any savings made by Hudson's schoolchildren. He eventually founded Ellsworth, Pennsylvania, a model coal mining town, and convinced JIC member Marshall Field to fund Chicago's Field Museum. An avid book collector who owned a copy of the Gutenberg Bible of 1455, Ellsworth's painting collection included the largest number of Innes landscapes in the world. In 1904 he purchased the "Villa Palmieri" near Florence, Italy, where Boccaccio wrote the *Decameron*. The villa dated back to 1336 and was formerly the home of Grand Duchess Marie de Bourbon. It also was owned by Lord Crawford who lent it on several occasions to Queen Victoria. Ellsworth's wife, Julia, died there in 1921. One of his daughters, Clare, was the wife of JIC member Bernon S. Prentice. Ellsworth contributed $100,000 to Roald Amundsen's airplane flight from the north coast of Norway to the North Pole in 1925 and his son, Lincoln, piloted one of the planes.

AMOS F. ENO (1837- 1915), merchant and banker. Eno was a silks and dress goods merchant when the Civil War broke out. He could not recover from the loss of his southern clients and went bankrupt. After serving as a colonel in the War he went back into business and eventually settled his previous debts thirty-six years later, although he was under no legal obligation to do so. Eno was a founder of the Second National Bank in New York City. He was unmarried and refused to have a telephone in his New York City home. When finally stricken, his servants could not call for help and had to go on foot to find a doctor. Eno was dead when the doctor arrived. His niece, Mary, married James W. Pinchot, and their sons were Amos Eno Pinchot, a New York City attorney who had a daughter, actress Rosamond (whose 1938 suicide shocked society), and son Gifford Pinchot, a forester who began the U.S.'s first systematic forest at Biltmore, North Carolina, then was governor of Pennsylvania 1923-27 and 1931-34.

GEORGE FRANCIS FABYAN (1837 - 1907), banker. A partner in the investment firm of Bliss, Fabyan & Company whose

Lincoln Ellsworth

Above: Aviator and explorer Lincoln Ellsworth, son of James, who completed the first transantarctic flight in history and piloted one of the airplanes on Amundsen's expedition to the North Pole. He named a mountain range there in honor of his father.

Right: James W. Ellsworth, philanthropist, who financed much of Amundsen's airplane flight from the coast of Norway to the North Pole in 1925.

New York City office was managed by JIC member Cornelius Bliss, Fabyan managed the firm in Boston. His yachts were the *Formosa* and the *Seneca.* His son, Francis W., was president of the Algonquin Club, a prominent Boston businessman and trustee of MIT who won sailing's Lipton Cup in 1906 and 1907. Another son, George, was a scientist who managed the family firm's office in Chicago.

NATHANIEL KELLOGG FAIRBANK (1829- 1904), manufacturer. As the head of N. K. Fairbank & Company of Chicago, he was one of the largest lard refiners and manufacturers of soap and cottonseed products in the world. One of his best-known lard products was "Cottolene." Fairbank was also a book publisher as well as one of the original trustees of the Chicago Symphony along with JIC member Ezra Butler McCagg. Fairbank, Arizona, was named for him because of his status as a major investor in the Grand Central Mining Company in nearby Tombstone. For many years he was president of the Chicago Club. Fairbank built a shingle style cottage at Jekyll in 1890 which was sold by his estate to Walton Ferguson and eventually demolished in 1944. He married Helen Livingston Graham and their son, Kellogg, was a Chicago lawyer who managed his father's estate. Their daughter, Helen Carpenter, was a supporter of Margaret Sanger's work.

HENRY FERGUSON (1848 - 1917), minister and professor. Ferguson was ordained as an Episcopal priest in 1873. He served as rector of St. Paul's School in Concord, New Hampshire, and was a professor at Trinity College in Hartford, Connecticut.

WALTON FERGUSON (1842 - 1922), developer. In 1878 Henry Clay Frick sold shares in Frick & Company to Edmund M.

Ferguson, then to his brother Walton Ferguson the following year, renaming the business H. C. Frick & Company. When Frick suffered a serious bout of inflammatory rheumatism, he stayed at Edmund M. Ferguson's house in Pittsburgh for a year while recovering. In 1886, the same year that Thomas Carnegie died, leaving his acreage on Georgia's Cumberland Island to his wife, Lucy, Leander Morris sold his Stafford land on Cumberland to Walton Ferguson. The next year, Walton Ferguson sold the Stafford land to Lucy Carnegie. Ferguson became president of the Stamford Gas Lighting Company in Connecticut. He implemented the merger of two local utilities and, in 1893, became president of the new Stamford Gas & Electric Company, capitalized at $500,000. Ferguson guided the company through the next twenty-four years of growth. In 1889, brothers Edmund M. and Walton Ferguson purchased almost all of Fishers Island, New York, for $250,000. He and his family then divided their time between Stamford and Fishers Island. In 1895 the Fergusons gave in memory of their second son, Edward (who died in 1890 at the age of 14), a stained glass window to St. John's Church in Stamford, Connecticut. The designer was Henry Edwards-Ficken, the architect who was later commissioned to design the Edward Ferguson memorial building at St. Luke's Chapel in South Stamford. Edwards-Ficken would become the supervising architect and engineer for Woodlawn Cemetery outside New York City.

WALTON FERGUSON, JR. (1870- 1936), auto dealer and dog breeder. Young Walton, who was president of the Stamford Motor Company, first married Emily Carstairs, daughter of a whiskey distiller. They separated in 1910 and he lived with his father on Fishers Island. Following a contentious divorce, he married Dorothy Herron Taylor in 1912. Ferguson was a well-known breeder of Springer spaniels and was president of the Westminster Kennel Club 1933-35.

GEORGE SPENCER FIELD (JIC member 1891-1897), bridge builder. A resident of Buffalo, Field became a partner in the Union Bridge Company with JIC members Stewart Maurice and Edmund Hayes. Among their constructions were the Cantilever Bridge over the Niagara (which he was credited with designing), the Cairo Bridge over the Ohio, and the Memphis Bridge over the Mississippi. Field later developed copper mines in Chile for the Guggenheim Corporation.

HENRY FIELD (JIC member from 1886; died 1890), salesman. The youngest brother of JIC member Marshall Field, Henry started as a clerk at Chicago's Cooley, Farwell and Company. When the company Field, Leiter was formed in 1867, Henry and his brother Joseph joined the new company as salesmen. Henry and his wife, Florence Lathrop, had three daughters before his death in 1890, leaving an estate of $2 million. The Art Institute of Chicago, officially dedicated in 1882, added lions flanking its doors in 1894, a gift from Mrs. Henry Field in honor of her late husband. Three years after his death his widow married the writer Thomas Nelson Page and they moved to Washington, D.C. and became active in Washington society. After his involvement in Woodrow Wilson's 1912 presidential campaign, Page was appointed ambassador to Italy in 1913, a position he held for six years. He died in 1922 at Oakland,

N. K. Fairbank became one of the largest lard refiners and manufacturers of soap in the world by making good use of early advertising.

his family's plantation in Hanover County, Virginia.

MARSHALL FIELD (1834 – 1906), department store founder. Born on a farm in Massachusetts, Field moved to Chicago at the age of nineteen and worked in a dry goods store, eventually rising to become a partner in the company. He and a partner, Levi Leiter (whose daughter would become Marchioness Curzon, Vicereine of India, second-highest ranking woman in the British Empire after Queen Victoria), joined another dry goods store owned by Potter Palmer. The new enterprise was known as Field, Palmer, and Leiter before Palmer retired from retailing. In 1881, Field bought out his remaining partner and changed the store's name to Marshall Field and Company. The quote "Give the lady what she wants" is attributed to him. The Field Museum of Natural History, named in his honor, was founded with his gift of $1,000,000 and was left an additional $8,000,000 at his death. He also gave land and $450,000 to the University of Chicago. His first marriage was to Nannie Douglass Scott in 1863. Their son, Marshall II (called "Junior"), was born in 1868 followed by daughter Ethel in 1873. Their Richard Morris Hunt-designed mansion on fashionable Prairie Avenue was Chicago's first to be wired for electricity. The marriage, however, was not happy and Nannie spent much of her time in Europe. She was rumored to be addicted to drugs and did not see her husband in later years except during his annual one-week visit to France. Their daughter, Ethel, married Arthur Tree and immediately moved to England. Her marriage was followed in 1890 by her brother's to the Catholic daughter of a German-born brewer, Albertine Huck (whose two sisters married Baron Komosky and Marquess Spinola).

Top: Marshall Field's flagship store in Chicago.

Bottom left: Marshall Field became famous as a merchant with the admonition, "Give the lady what she wants."

Bottom right: The Field residence on fashionable Prairie Avenue was Chicago's first to be wired for electricity.

Although the marriage was happy, it was not one his parents had hoped for and the young couple followed his sister to live in England. Within two years their mother moved permanently to France where she died in 1896. Two years later daughter Ethel, having had a son, Ronald Tree, began a relationship with David Beatty, the youngest admiral in the royal navy, whom she married in 1901 ten days after being divorced by her husband for desertion. Beatty was later created an Earl for his heroism in the Battle of Jutland. While Ethel enjoyed their high social profile, the marriage was unhappy although it produced the required heir to inherit the Earldom (he married Americans three times). Her granddaughter is the current Viscountess Gage. Ethel's brother, Junior, and his wife had two sons, Marshall III and Henry, and a daughter, Gwendolyn. The senior Field's trips to England to see his grandchildren became more frequent and it was in London that he married in 1905 Mrs. Delia Spencer Caton, a long-time neighbor in Chicago whom many suspected of having been his mistress for decades (her late husband, who died the year before, owned all the telegraph lines in Illinois and Iowa). The families of both his children accompanied the couple back to Chicago for their honeymoon. There, only six weeks later, Marshall II was fatally injured by a handgun while alone in his room. His father, who was in New York at the time, rushed home to his side but the son died five days later. There was no autopsy and his family insisted the death was accidental although most presumed suicide. Six weeks later, his grief-stricken father developed pneumonia after playing golf in the snow and died after several days' struggle. His will left approximately $140,000,000 ($2.6 billion in twenty-first century dollars) with the majority in trust to his two grandsons with the elder, Marshall III, receiving $72,000,000 and his brother $48,000,000. The younger son, Henry, married in 1917 Nancy Perkins, daughter of the eldest of the famed Langhorne sisters and a niece of Lady Astor. Five months later he was dead after an operation to remove his tonsils, leaving the vast Field estate to his elder brother (although a lawsuit over inheritance rights of Henry's illegitimate son continued for years). Henry's widow, Nancy, then married Ronald Tree, her husband's first cousin, who was a son of Ethel Beatty's first marriage. After her divorce from Tree she was married to Claude Lancaster and became known as the noted tastemaker Nancy Lancaster, owner of Sybil Colefax & John Fowler, a British decorating firm known for its "English country-house look." She lived until 1994 at the age of ninety-seven, when her body was returned to Virginia to be buried with her first husband, Henry Field. Marshall III first married Evelyn Marshall by whom he had Marshall IV and two daughters, then married Audrey James Coats, a god-daughter (and, some said, daughter) of King Edward VII and former fiancée of Lord Louis Mountbatten, and finally Ruth Pruyn Phipps. Ruth, formerly the wife of his friend Ogden Phipps, was a granddaughter of JIC member Robert Pruyn (Ruth and Marshall III were close friends and financial supporters of Eleanor Roosevelt). Both of the daughters by the last marriage would take their own life. Marshall III and Henry's younger sister, Gwendolyn, married Sir Archibald Edmonstone, 3rd Baronet. Their daughter, Alyssa, married in 1999 His Royal and Imperial Highness Prince

Sigismund, head of the Grand Ducal House of Tuscany and Grand Duke of Austria and Bohemia and Prince of Hungary. They have a daughter and two sons, one of whom will presumably succeed his father as head of the royal house. Marshall Field & Company built Chicago's Merchandise Mart in 1931, at the time the world's largest building, containing over four million square feet of floor space. In 1945, with Field's wholesale business in decline, the Merchandise Mart was sold to Joseph P. Kennedy, father of President John F. Kennedy. Marshall Field's department store chain was acquired by Target in 1990, sold to Macy's Department Stores in 2004, and was purchased by Federated Department Stores in 2005.

NEWTON SOBIESKI FINNEY (1835-1910), commission and shipping merchant. Finney was appointed to West Point but resigned after he was unable to master his academics. He was given a surveying position with the Coast Guard and was assigned to chart Georgia's Brunswick harbor, along with neighboring St. Simons Island. There he met his wife, Josephine du Bignon, whose family eventually owned all of Jekyll Island. At the outbreak of the Civil War he volunteered for the Confederacy even though his family members in the North were fighting for the Union. Through speculation he amassed a small fortune during the War but it was wiped out with the defeat of the South and his home and contents were confiscated. He entered a New York shipping and commission merchant firm with eventual JIC member Oliver Kane King under the name of King, Finney & Company and moved his family to New York City, where he joined the powerful Union Club. With his brother-in-law, John Eugene du Bignon, Finney developed

Jekyll Island by brokering in 1886 the purchase of Jekyll Island for $125,000 from his wife's family. Finney personally solicited memberships from the most powerful businessmen of the day and is credited with having founded the Jekyll Island Club.

LATHAM AVERY FISH (1842 - 1909), yachtsman. Fish served as a sergeant in the Hawkins Zouaves and was president of the Shelter Island Golf Club. In 1883, while serving as commodore of the Atlantic Yacht Club, he commissioned a schooner yacht he named the *Grayling*. He died at his summer home in Greenport, Long Island.

HENRY JOHNSON FISHER (1873 -1965), publisher. Fisher was chairman of the McCall Corporation until his retirement in 1945, founder and chairman of the board of Popular Science Publishing Company, and chairman of the executive committee of Harper Brothers. He and his wife, Alice Agnew, and their family lived in Greenwich, Connecticut. The Magazine Publishers of America gives an annual award for excellence named for Fisher.

PLINY FISK (1860 - 1939), broker. An early associate of J. P. Morgan, Fisk was head of his family's investment firm, Harvey Fisk & Sons. In 1901 he made $800,000 overnight by calling the financial bluff of E. H. Harriman, who was trying to break the government bond market. Fisk underwrote the funds for digging a train tunnel under the Hudson River. He had a nervous breakdown in 1919 and retired, selling his New York Stock Exchange seat for $55,000. In 1924 he was forced by financial necessity to sell his estate in Rye, New York, his steam yacht, the *Riviera*, and to resign his many clubs. He moved into a single room and J. P. Morgan continued to send him $100 per month. Fisk died in the Home for Incurables.

CHARLES ROBERT FORREST (1842- 1912), director. Forrest, a resident of Hartford, Connecticut, was a director of the Connecticut River Lumber Company and other corporations.

WILLIAM DUDLEY FOULKE (1848 - 1935), attorney and author. A native of Richmond, Indiana, Foulke was an Indiana state senator before being appointed a U. S. civil service commissioner by President Theodore Roosevelt. An early women's suffragist, his funeral was conducted by his eldest grandson, the Rev.William Dudley Foulke Hughes, precentor of the Cathedral of St. John the Divine in New York City. Foulke wrote *A Hoosier's Autobiography*, as well as several other books.

CHILDS FRICK (1883 - 1965), paleontologist and steel heir. The only son of "the King of Coke," Henry Clay Frick, he led numerous scientific expeditions around the world and was the author of *Horned Ruminants of North America*. Frick served as a trustee of the American Museum of Natural History from 1921 until his death and established its Frick Laboratory of Vertebrate Paleontology. In 1912 he led an expedition to Abyssinia and was a trustee of the New York Zoological Society. He was president of the board of the Frick Collection from 1921 until his death as well as a director of the Mellon National Bank. Just prior to his 1913 wedding to Frances Dixon, Frick's father gave him $12 million and, afterwards, presented his new daughter-in-law with an envelope containing a $2 million check. They lived at "Clayton" in Roslyn, New York, where he died. Frick's daughter, Frances, married Townsend Burden, Jr.

Above: Clayton, the Childs Frick residence in Roslyn, Long Island.

Bottom: Marshall Field III, whose immense inheritance did not shield him from unhappiness.

Left: May Goelet was such a prized heiress that the reprobate 9th Duke of Manchester announced his engagement to her as a tactic to keep his creditors at bay. Instead, in one of the few "love matches" of the era, she married in 1903 the 8th Duke of Roxburghe.

Above: The 8th Duke of Roxburghe whose Floors Castle was expensively refurbished by Goelet money. The current Prince Andrew, Duke of York, and his former wife, Sarah Ferguson, became engaged there.

Another daughter, Martha, married Fife Symington and their son became governor of Arizona before being convicted in 1997 of multiple counts of fraud, extortion, and perjury. The Fricks' only son, Henry Clay Frick II, was a gynecologist who remained active on the board of the Frick Collection.

WALTER ROGERS FURNESS (1861- 1914), sportsman. From a socially prominent Philadelphia family, Furness was the youngest original member of the Club. He learned of Jekyll from his mother's brother, JIC member Fairman Rogers. Furness left Harvard in his senior year when he inherited a substantial estate from his maternal grandfather. He briefly worked for the architectural firm of his uncle, Frank Furness. In 1890 he built his own cottage at Jekyll and used it frequently with his family and guests. He was a keen hunter but lost interest in Jekyll when he sustained an eye injury and was no longer able to enjoy the sport. In 1896 he sold his cottage to Joseph Pulitzer who used it to house servants until his own home on the island was completed (the Furness cottage later became the Club's infirmary). Furness died only one month after his wife. His son, Fairman, served at the U. S. Embassy in Russia.

EDWARD STANLEY GARY (1862 -), cotton manufacturer. Gary's father was postmaster general in the administration of President McKinley, a close family friend and frequent visitor to the Gary home in Baltimore. Gary was president, then chairman of the board of James S. Gary & Son, cotton manufacturers. He was president of the Baltimore Board of Trade and lived in Catonsville near Baltimore.

MICHAEL GAVIN (1872 - 1960), attorney and banker. A Memphis native, Gavin married in 1906 in St. Paul, Minnesota, Gertrude Hill, daughter of JIC member James J. Hill. He practiced law in New York City, then became a partner in an investment firm there before retiring in 1928. Gertrude Hill Gavin was the first president of the National Council for Catholic Women for which she was decorated by the Pope in 1924. She died six months after her husband and left her forty-five acre estate, including a home with thirty-six rooms and a chapel, in Oyster Bay, Long Island, to the nation as a residence for the U. S. Ambassador to the United Nations. There were no children.

OGDEN GOELET (1846-1897), estate executor. One of two sons of Robert Goelet II and Sarah Ogden, he was a brother of JIC member Robert Goelet III. He served as a trustee of Chemical Bank and Trust Company but came into a huge inheritance from his unmarried uncle, Peter Goelet, who was known to be so stingy that he mended his own clothes rather than pay a tailor. At his large town house, the uncle kept pheasants, peacocks, and cows that he milked himself. His estate of approximately $30 million (in 1879) allowed his nephew to live in great style with his very social wife, Mary Wilson. She was one of the "Marrying Wilsons" of Georgia who were known for their fortunate marriages. Mary's brother received a half million dollars from his father when he married a daughter of "the" Mrs. Astor. The Wilson sisters married Cornelius Vanderbilt and Sir Mungo Herbert, later the British Ambassador to the U. S. The Goelets' Newport mansion, "Ochre Court," designed by Richard Morris Hunt and built at an expense of

Society beauty Mrs. Robert Goelet IV.

$4.5 million, enabled them to entertain guests such as Grand Duke Boris of Russia in great style. The Ogden Goelets ascended to the highest levels of society when their only daughter, May, married the young 8th Duke of Roxburghe. Even though it was considered a "love match" (despite her having brought a $20 million inheritance to the marriage), her compatriot Consuelo Vanderbilt, Duchess of Marlborough (their husbands were cousins), said of May that her "chief interests were needlework, salmon fishing and bridge. To these diversions she devoted a good brain which might perhaps have been used to better purpose." They were old friends (May was a bridesmaid in Consuelo's wedding) but, while May's marriage to her duke was a happy one, Consuelo's was not. The current Duke of Roxburghe is May's grandson.

ROBERT GOELET III (1841-1899), non-practicing attorney. He and his brother, Ogden, inherited a vast fortune that included 259 houses in the middle of Manhattan. Robert's wife was Harriette Warren, whose first cousin, Phillips Phoenix, was a JIC member. Harriette Warren Goelet's brother, Whitney, was a well-known society architect, and their sister, Edith, married William Starr Miller (the Carrere and Hastings-designed Miller mansion still stands at 5th Avenue and 86th Street; the Miller's daughter married Baron Queenborough). Robert managed his family's extensive real estate holdings. He had a mansion on 5th Avenue as well as an estate in Tuxedo Park, and his Newport estate, "Southside," was partially designed by Stanford White. After his death, his wife traveled on their yacht, the *Nahma*, to Paris to be treated for cancer. She died there in 1914, only a few months after she had entertained on her yacht at different times the Emperor and the Crown Princess of Germany. Her estate, in excess of $3 million, was left to their son, JIC member Robert Walton Goelet.

ROBERT GOELET IV (1880 - 1966), estate director and yachtsman. He was a son of JIC member Ogden Goelet and a first cousin of JIC member Robert Walton Goelet. He inherited his parents' fifty-room Newport mansion, "Ochre Court," which required (during a typical eight-week summer season) twenty-seven house servants, eight coachmen and grooms, and twelve gardeners. They moved into the smaller "Champ Soleil" and in 1947 deeded "Ochre Court" to the Sisters of Mercy to establish Salve Regina College. Goelet served as a director of Chemical Bank and of New York Trust Company. His first marriage was to the beautiful but poor Elsie Whelen (after their divorce she married Newport socialite Henry Clews). Goelet's second marriage, to Fernanda Rocci Raibouchinsky, was not recognized by his mother and she would not return to Newport until her son's third marriage to Roberta Willard. His daughter married James E. Cross, son of JIC member Elliott Cross. His sons were Ogden II, Peter IV, and Robert V.

ROBERT WALTON GOELET (1880 - 1941), non-practicing attorney and executor of father's estate. He was a son of JIC member Robert III and Harriette Warren Goelet and a nephew of JIC member Ogden Goelet. His only sibling, Beatrice, died in 1902 leaving him sole heir to their father's $60 million estate. He greatly resembled his first cousin, JIC member Robert Goelet, who was born in the same year, so he was nicknamed "Bertie" at a young age

to distinguish the two. They jointly graduated from Harvard in 1902 and received their masters degrees there the following year. In addition to his other homes, he maintained an apartment in Paris, a fishing lodge on the Restigouche River in Canada, and a castle at Sandricourt twenty-five miles outside of Paris. Built in 1908 by the Marquis de Beauvoir, it comprised ten thousand acres, had 139 buildings and was taken over by the Germans during World War II. In 1921 Goelet married Anne Guestier, whose father was one of the wealthiest wine merchants in France and an ardent horse breeder. Goelet's will left the Ritz-Carlton Hotel in New York City and its site free and clear of mortgage to Harvard. His yacht, the *Nahma*, was given to the U. S. Navy for use during World War I.

FRANK HENRY GOODYEAR (1849 - 1907), manufacturer. From a modest background, he began his career as a teacher. In 1871 he married Josephine, daughter of Robert Looney of Looneyville, Pennsylvania, a saw mill operator who started Goodyear in business. With his older brother, Charles, in 1887 he founded the Goodyear Lumber Company. He was also president of the Susquehanna Coal Company and president and chairman of the Buffalo & Susquehanna Railroad Company. Goodyear later organized the Great Southern Lumber Company in Louisiana as well as the New Orleans Great Northern Railroad Company. In 1903 Goodyear contracted with the architectural firm of Carrere and Hastings, who also designed his home in Buffalo, to design his cottage at Jekyll. Both were ready for his family in 1906 but he enjoyed them less than a year before his death. His son, Frank, Jr., was a JIC member, as was the husband of Florence Goodyear,

Charles Meldrum Daniels. The other Goodyear daughter, Grace, married as her second husband Howard Potter, son of the influential Episcopal Bishop of New York, Henry C. Potter, who was the step-father of JIC member Stephen C. Clark.

FRANK HENRY GOODYEAR, JR. (1891- 1930), manufacturer. Goodyear worked in his family's lumber and railroad businesses and organized and headed the Goodyear-Wende Oil Company of Buffalo, distributor of thirty-six Texaco service stations. In 1915 he married Dorothy Knox and they made frequent use of the Goodyear cottage at Jekyll, which he inherited. In 1930 he purchased the Furness cottage at Jekyll and donated it to the Club as an infirmary in memory of his mother. He also brought his yacht, the *Poule d'Eau,* to Jekyll but in 1929, while anchored offshore at Miami, it was demolished in an explosion that killed its engineer. Goodyear also inherited his parents' home in Buffalo and built another in East Aurora. In 1930 he was driving his Rolls Royce with his wife and other passengers, including JIC member Bernon Prentice, in the car when he crashed into a tree. Although the passengers escaped with only minor injuries, Goodyear was killed. Eleven months later, his widow (with four small children) married JIC member Edmund Rogers, a widower who had been their next-door neighbor at Jekyll. One of the Goodyear daughters, Marjorie, married a son of JIC member Hope Norman Bacon.

JOSEPHINE LOONEY GOODYEAR (Mrs. Frank Henry Goodyear) (1851 -1915). She was a daughter of Robert Looney of Looneyville, Pennsylvania, a saw mill operator who started Frank H. Goodyear in the lumber business. She founded the Josephine Goodyear Convalescent Home for Children in Buffalo and, in 1909, was elected a JIC member in her own right. The Infirmary at Jekyll was donated by her son in her memory.

EDWIN GOULD (1866- 1933), railroad executive and financier. Edwin was Jay Gould's second son who, unlike his elder brother, George, placed hard work and family harmony above social pursuits. Consequently he, almost alone of the Gould family, had a happy marriage while simultaneously greatly increasing his inherited fortune. He was president of the "Cotton Belt" railroad, the St. Louis Southwestern, before becoming its chairman. He founded and was president of the Continental Match Company and was a trustee of his father's $84 million estate. He founded the Edwin Gould Foundation for Children and left it half his fortune at his death. Gould married in 1892 Sarah Cantine, stepdaughter of JIC member Dr. George Shrady. In 1900 Gould bought David H. King's Jekyll home, renamed "Chicota," and immediately began adapting and updating it for use by his family. He added a private wharf and boathouse as well as a bowling alley and covered tennis court. Their yacht was the *Nada* and their private railroad car the *Dixie.* At his encouragement, his parents-in-law became JIC members and built their own home at Jekyll. Both his sons, Edwin, Jr., and Frank Miller Gould, would become JIC members, although both died young. The Goulds' Jekyll home was demolished in 1941.

EDWIN GOULD, JR. (1893 - 1917). The eldest son of JIC member Edwin Gould, he was elected a JIC member in 1914 when he was twenty-one. Young Gould was never academically gifted and may well have been learning disabled. He loved the freedom

offered by Jekyll and was close to his maternal grandparents, JIC members Dr. and Mrs. George Shrady. His father bought the marshy island known as Latham Hammock overlooking Jekyll on the mainland side to help maintain the splendid isolation offered by the Club. On February 24, 1917, Edwin, Jr. was killed in an accident at Jekyll when he was hunting on Latham Hammock, accompanied by the tutor of the family of fellow JIC member Tracy Dows. His gun accidentally discharged into his body when he struck its butt against a raccoon caught in a trap. As a result of their grief, his mother never again set foot on Jekyll and his father did so only after an absence of four years.

FRANK MILLER GOULD (1899 - 1945), railroad executive. The younger son of JIC member Edwin Gould and grandson of Jay Gould, he served as vice president of the St. Louis Southwestern Railway, a road developed by his grandfather. He continued his father's chief philanthropic interest by becoming chairman of the board of the Edwin Gould Foundation for Children. Gould also owned prize steeplechase horses. He married in Dallas, Texas, in 1924, Florence Bacon, niece of the president of his railroad. They had a son, Edwin Jay, and a daughter, Marianne, for whom Villa Mariana, his home at Jekyll constructed in 1928, was named; he divorced in May of 1944. While serving as a Captain in the Air Force and stationed in Macon, Georgia, Gould married divorcee Helen

Mrs. George Gould and her famous pearls. At this point she still possessed her famous hourglass figure. When the sands ran to the bottom, so did her husband's ardor. He was quietly dropped from Jekyll's membership rolls when knowledge of his mistress and their illegitimate children became public.

Roosen Curran, who had a daughter and son of her own. They honeymooned at Jekyll's Villa Mariana and he was the best financial hope for preventing the Club's closing. He was working with JIC member Bill Jones to form a syndicate for Jekyll's continuation when, only seven months after his second marriage, he died of a heart attack at the age of forty-five. At his death his two children shared a $7 million trust fund established by their grandfather, a separate trust fund from their grandmother, as well as $14,000 each annually from a trust fund set up by their father for their mother.

GEORGE JAY GOULD (1864 - 1923), railroad executive. The eldest son of financier Jay Gould, he inherited several of the executive positions of his father as the elder Gould began relinquishing duties in his later years. He married in 1886 an amateur actress, Edith Kingdon, known for her hour-glass figure and famous pearls, and they lived at "Georgian Court" in Lakewood, New Jersey. Among their seven children (one of whom was born on her father's yacht, the *Atalanta*) were nationally-ranked tennis player Jay Gould II and Vivien Gould, who married the 5th Baron Decies. The Decies' grandson is the current Baron. George Jay Gould allied himself with John D. Rockefeller and Andrew Carnegie against the interests of JIC member J. P. Morgan. At the height of his family's power, he and his five siblings were each receiving $115,000 per week from their varied interests, all at a time before there was an income tax. But the son was not the father and George continued depleting not only his

Top: George Gould's legitimate children. There were an additional three by his mistress whom he married after his wife's death. Bottom: George Gould with two of his daughters, Edith and Gloria. Another daughter, Vivien, in 1911 married the 5th Baron Decies.

own fortune but those of his siblings, several of whom eventually sued him for malfeasance. His wife, whose girth increased with each year of marriage, died of a heart attack in 1921 while playing golf on the private Gould course at "Georgian Court." The stays in her girdle could not be loosened sufficiently to allow her to breathe and she was dead before the doctors could reach her. Gould's membership at Jekyll was allowed to expire when it became public that he kept an acknowledged mistress, Guinevere Sinclair, and three illegitimate children while his wife was still alive. His yacht was frequently moored at the mansion in Rye, New York, that he purchased for them. After Edith's death, Gould married Guinevere, although their children were not allowed to share in his vast estate. He died at Cap Martin, near Mentone, from an illness begun as a cold caught in the Valley of the Kings in Egypt which he visited after the discovery of King Tut's tomb. After his death, Guinevere married Viscount Dunsford, later 2nd Earl of Midleton, and he was disinherited by his family. George's younger siblings had secured a $50 million judgment against him for mismanaging their estates but they eventually settled for $20 million shortly before he died. Only then was it discovered that his estate contained only $15 million and was eventually reduced by taxes and legal costs to $5 million to divide among his heirs. Gould's youngest sister, Anna, was one of the most famous heiresses to marry a fortune to a title. She first married Count Boniface de Castellane, Proust's model for the dandy Saint-Loup, who spent millions of her dollars before she divorced him and married his cousin, Helie de Talleyrand-Perigord, Prince de Sagan, 5th Duc de Talleyrand.

HUGH JOHN GRANT (1855 - 1910), real estate developer and mayor. Grant made a fortune in real estate. After serving as an alderman and sheriff, he was elected for two terms as mayor of New York City 1889 - 1892 (he had first been nominated for mayor in 1884 when he was only thirty-one). An influential member of Tammany Hall and prominent Catholic, he attempted to be re-elected mayor in 1894, but was defeated and retired from politics. He dropped on the steps of his home and died of a heart attack. In 1911, Hugh Grant Circle in the Bronx was named for him and still commemorates his service as mayor.

JULIE M. MURPHY GRANT (Mrs. Hugh John Grant) (JIC member 1912-1919; died 1944). Mrs. Grant continued as a member in her own right. She died at their New York City home leaving a son, Hugh, and daughters Julia and Edna.

GEORGE EDWARD GRAY (1818- 1913), engineer. Gray was vice president and director of the Wells-Fargo Express Company. He became chief engineer of the New York Railroad in 1853 and was a trustee of Stanford. He married Lucina Corning of Syracuse.

JAMES BROWN MASON GROSVENOR (JIC member from 1886; died 1905), merchant. Grosvenor was a New York City merchant and a breeder of prize horses. He married Minna Ludeling, daughter of a Louisiana judge, and they had a summer home in Newport. After her husband's death she bought a summer camp in the Laurentian Forest near Murray Bay, Quebec, and died in 1916.

WALTER SUFFERN GURNEE (1813-1903), manufacturer and mayor. Originally from New York State, Gurnee moved to

Detroit then to Chicago in 1836 where he became a successful manufacturer, merchant, and banker. He was heavily invested in construction and the early development of railroads in the Chicago area. Gurnee was elected mayor of Chicago in 1851 and served two terms. Winnetka and Highland Park were developed on his land and the town of Gurnee, Illinois, was named in his honor when the Chicago, Milwaukee and St. Paul Railroad, on whose board he served, was built through the town. He was a close friend and supporter of Stephen Douglas. In 1863 he returned to New York and purchased an estate near Irvington, Westchester County. Gurnee's son, Walter, Jr., married Bella Barney and was a New York City broker whose home was at "Belespoir" in Westbury, Long Island.

WILLIAM DAMERON GUTHRIE (1859 -1935), attorney. His father had been Surveyor of the Port of San Francisco and owned several California newspapers. Guthrie spent his childhood in France and attended college in England. He was a partner in the law firm of Steward, Guthrie & Steele until he retired in 1902 to become a member of J. P. Morgan & Company. Guthrie was counsel for the Catholic Church, including his appearance before the U. S. Supreme Court in 1929 on behalf of the Archbishop of Manila. He was honored for his work by the French government and by the pope. Guthrie was elected the first mayor of Lattingtown, New York, in 1931 and was re-elected in 1933. His 350-acre home was "Muedon" on the north shore of Long Island. John W. Davis, former Democratic nominee for president, was visiting him at the time of his heart attack and was the first to reach

him before his death.

HAMILTON HADDEN (1885 – 1963), polo player. A son of J. E. Smith Hadden (his mother was a Hamilton), he lived with his family at Uniondale Farm in Hempstead, Long Island. Following his graduation from Harvard, he was a well-known polo player for Meadow Brook. In 1913 he married Anita Peabody who died in 1960. Their son, Hamilton, Jr., was an attorney who was a partner at the New York law firm of Shearman and Sterling and served as general counsel of Chemstrand Corporation.

JOHN LOOMER HALL (1872 - 1960), attorney. Hall's father was president of the New York, New Haven & Hartford Railroad Company. The son, who graduated from Yale, was prominent in the reorganization of the same railway after its bankruptcy and served as one of its trustees. He was a partner with Charles F. Choate in Choate & Hall. On the day of his death, Hall traveled to New Haven to see his son, Edward Tuck Hall, headmaster of the Hill School in Pottstown, Pennsylvania, receive a master of arts degree from Yale. He became ill and died at the home of a relative only hours before the ceremony.

JOHN HENRY HAMMOND (1871 -1949), attorney. His father, Gen. John Hammond, was chief of staff to Gen. William T. Sherman during the Civil War then became "the father of Superior, Wisconsin" for having transformed swampland into a thriving city. Hammond's maternal grandfather was Nathaniel Wolfe, former attorney general of the state of Kentucky. Originally from Minneapolis, Hammond graduated from Yale and was a partner in the New York law firm of Dorr, Hammond, Hand, & Dawson. He lived in New York City and at "Dellwood" in Mt. Kisco, New York. Hammond married in 1899 Emily V. Sloane, a granddaughter of William H. Vanderbilt. He served as counsel for the Frick Collection and a director of W & J Sloane Company. He was deputy attorney general of New York State 1899 – 1901 and was in charge of a case bringing charges against the district attorney of New York County and his subsequent removal from office. Hammond then became a partner in the law firm of Cadwalader, Wickersham & Taft, and later a partner in the banking firm Brown Brothers, Harriman & Company. At the time of Hammond's death, he was playing in the U. S. Senior Golf Tournament at the Apawamis Club and had just stepped onto the tenth green when he collapsed and died. On the day of his funeral a memorial service in honor of Hammond as a pioneer industrial statesman was held in Switzerland with delegates from forty-two countries at the World Assembly for Moral Re-Armament. One of Hammond's daughters, Alice, married musician Benny Goodman. The Hammonds' son, John, Jr., was active in the NAACP. He was a record producer who discovered Bessie Smith, Billie Holiday, Bob Dylan, and Bruce Springsteen and was the father of musician John Hammond. The JIC member's brother, Ogden, was the U. S. Ambassador to Spain. Ogden and his wife, heiress Mary Stevens, were on the *Lusitania* when it was sunk. Even though they had been warned by the German Ambassador not to take this particular journey, Mary Hammond refused to cancel their trip, and, on the night before sailing, John H. Hammond drew up a will for his sister-in-law which she signed on the ship just prior to departure. Although Ogden survived, his wife died after their lifeboat dropped

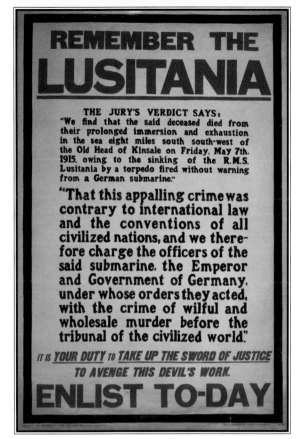

Top: The Lusitania's sinking caused the death of many society figures including Mary Hammond, who had been warned by the German Ambassador not to sail on this particular journey.

Bottom: Musician Benny Goodman was the son-in-law of Jekyll member John H. Hammond. Record producer John Hammond, Jr. discovered Bessie Smith and Billie Holliday and launched the careers of Bob Dylan and Bruce Springsteen.

sixty feet into the water. Ogden Hammond's daughters were Mary "Ma" Hammond who married Count Ghino Roberti, Italy's ambassador to Mexico, and Millicent Hammond Fenwick, U. S. Congresswoman from New Jersey then U. S. representative, with the rank of ambassador, to the United Nations Agencies for Food and Agriculture 1983-87. John H. Hammond's brother-in-law, Lincoln MacVeagh, was the U.S. Minister to Greece, Iceland, and South Africa and the Ambassador to Yugoslavia, Greece, Portugal, and Spain.

DOROTHEA BARNEY HARDING (Mrs. James Horace Harding) (1871-1935). She was a daughter of banker Charles Dennis Barney and Laura Elmina Cooke, and granddaughter of banker Jay Cooke, financier for the Union whose sale of bonds provided the Union Army with a generous amount of funding, eventually enabling the Union victory. She married JIC member James H. Harding in 1898. They lived at 955 Fifth Avenue in New York City.

JAMES HORACE HARDING (1863 - 1929), financier. Harding's father owned the *Philadelphia Inquirer*. The son was a partner in Charles D. Barney & Company, investment bankers, and managed its New York City branch. Among his clients were Edward H. Harriman, Henry C. Frick, and William Rockefeller. Harding was chairman of the board of American Express Company and a director of many corporations. He owned the corner of Broadway and Wall Street and developed it as the site of the headquarters of American Exchange-Irving Trust Bank. Harding was the executor of the extensive estate of Jay Cooke, his wife's

grandfather. He donated part of the right of way for Nassau Boulevard to be built for access to the north shore points on Long Island and, after his death, it was renamed in his memory. Harding was treasurer and trustee of the Frick Collection. His daughter, Catharine, married Lorillard Suffern Tailer, grandson of JIC member Pierre Lorillard. A Harding great-granddaughter, Hilary King, married Herbert Peter Pulitzer, grandson of JIC member Joseph Pulitzer, whose second wife, Roxanne, wrote the scandalous account of their marriage, *The Prize Pulitzer*. His first wife, with whom he eloped, was the designer Lilly Pulitzer, step-daughter of steel heir Ogden Phipps whose wife, Ruth, was a granddaughter of JIC member Robert Pruyn and the third wife of Marshall Field III.

EDWARD STEPHEN HARKNESS (1874 - 1940), philanthopist. His father, Stephen, was an original partner in Standard Oil with John D. Rockefeller. In Rockefeller's worst financial crisis of his early career, Harkness contributed his entire life savings of $70,000 to keep the company afloat. Harkness subsequently became the largest Rockefeller partner. Another of Rockefeller's partners was William M. Flagler, who married Harkness' niece. Harkness received doctorates of divinity from The University of St. Andrews in Scotland and from Columbia University. He was a trustee of the Metropolitan Museum of Art and a director of the Southern Pacific Company as well the Central Railroad Lines. Although Harkness had no children, he was sole heir to his father and brother who pre-deceased him and from whom he inherited more than $200 million. When his mother died in 1926 leaving him an additional $30 million, he continued

Top left: Edward S. Harkness became one of Yale's most generous benefactors, contributing funds to build its first eight residential dormitories.

Bottom left: Harkness Tower is one of the most recognized landmarks on Yale's campus.

Bottom: Dorothea Barney (later Mrs. James Harding), with her father (on the left), Charles D. Barney and Rev. Lorin Webster.

Philanthropist Edward S. Harkness. In one ten-year period his known gifts exceeded $55 million. He donated the land for Columbia Presbyterian Hospital, gave the institution $47 million outright, and left it an additional bequest in his will.

her charities and began his own as well. The inheritance taxes paid by his mother and brother were among the top five ever paid in the U.S. until that time. He had a 135-foot diesel yacht, *Stevana*, which he used to commute to work. Although his gifts were usually anonymous, he was known to have contributed at least $100 million during his lifetime and much more than that amount in his will. Yale, which he attended, was one of his largest beneficiaries but many other institutions received major funds as well. In one ten-year period his known gifts totaled more than $55 million. He gave Stillman Hall (having married Mary Stillman in 1904) to Colgate in memory of his father-in-law.

One of the most identifiable landmarks of the Yale campus, Harkness Tower, is part of the Memorial Quadrangle completed in 1921 as a gift of his mother. In that same year, Edward S. Harkness and his mother donated twenty-two acres in Washington Heights to Columbia University and Presbyterian Hospital as the site for the new medical center. At the time of its establishment he contributed $47 million with an additional bequest in his will. Harkness also gave Egyptian antiquities to the Metropolitan Museum, having been present at the opening of the third shrine in the tomb of King Tut at Luxor in Egypt. He and his wife lived at "Eolia" in New London, Connecticut, and had a home in Manhattan. His wife's family property was preserved as Mystic Seaport, Connecticut. She gave Yale a Gutenberg Bible and gave a dormitory and chapel to Connecticut College as well as a women's dormitory to Oberlin College. At her death she left $60 million to the Commonwealth Fund and other beneficiaries. The Commonwealth Fund was founded by her mother-in-law and today grants funds for health care services from a corpus of more than $600 million.

DWIGHT MILLER HARRIS (1859 - 1903), broker. Harris lived in Lakewood, New Jersey, and was a broker in the City. He was a nephew of the Jay Goulds through Mrs. Gould, and was thus a cousin of JIC members George Gould and Edwin Gould. He entertained his cousins, Count and Countess Boniface de Castellane (she was Anna Gould) at his New Jersey estate in 1900. He died at his New York home at the age of forty-four.

THOMAS SKELTON HARRISON (1837 - 1919), manufacturer and diplomat. During the Civil War he served as paymaster of the U. S. Navy. He became a partner at Philadelphia's Harrison Brothers, owners of the Pennsylvania Sugar Refinery, where he became president in 1902. Harrison often traveled to Egypt where he was decorated by the Khedive. In 1897 President McKinley appointed him diplomatic agent and U. S. Consul General to the Court of the Khedive, a position he held for two years before resigning to become president of Harrison Brothers. He and his wife, Louise, lived in Philadelphia and had no children.

EDWIN HAWLEY (1850 - 1912), railway president. Hawley began his career in the freight department of the Rock Island Railroad and was spotted by Collis P. Huntington who hired him. He eventually became president of the Chesapeake and Ohio as well as the Iowa Central and the Minneapolis & St. Louis Railroads. He was a director of forty-one corporations. Although an early ally of E. H. Harriman, Hawley broke with him and sided with the Gould interests in the building of the Western Pacific. A bachelor,

Hawley left an estate of $50 million. In his obituary, the *New York Times* remarked, "He had friendships but no affections."

EDMUND B. HAYES (1849-1923), civil engineer and manufacturer. Brigadier General Hayes was a pioneer investor in the development of electrical power from Niagara Falls. His company built the steel arch bridge at Niagara Falls and installed the first power plant on the Canadian side of the river. He was a personal friend of Grover Cleveland who made him a general in the national guard while he was president. He and his business partner, JIC member John J. Albright, formed the Lackawanna Steel Company. Hayes Hall was named in honor of his bequest to the University of Buffalo. JIC members George S. Field and Stewart Maurice were his partners in the Union Bridge Company which not only built bridges but also manufactured autos.

BAYARD HENRY (1857 -1926), attorney and railroad president. A Philadelphia lawyer, Henry was president of the United New Jersey Railroad & Canal Company, a director of the Pennsylvania Railroads and other corporations. He was a member of the Pennsylvania State Senate 1898-1902 and a trustee of Princeton University from which he graduated in 1876. He died in San Francisco and left extensive historical documents and correspondence to his alma mater where a graduate fellowship is still named in his honor.

JANE IRWIN ROBESON HENRY (Mrs. Bayard Henry) (JIC member 1931-34). She and her husband lived in Germantown. In 1929 she gave a collection of historical documents relating to Princeton to her husband's alma mater. She took over her

husband's JIC Club share after his estate held it until 1931.

PARMELY WEBB HERRICK (1881 - 1937), banker and broker. He was a son of Myron T. Herrick who was governor of Ohio 1903-06 and ambassador to France 1912-1914. The son was a partner in the securities firm of Hayden, Stone & Company of New York City, having been a banker and realtor in his native Cleveland.   Herrick graduated from Harvard in 1904 and two years later married Agnes Blackwell of St. Louis. He was president of the Herrick Company and was decorated by the governments of France and Belgium. Herrick was a friend of Charles Lindbergh, who visited him in Cleveland after his trans-Atlantic flight. Parmely Herrick had lent Lindbergh a suit on the day after his arrival in Paris where he was greeted by Ambassador Herrick, and Lindbergh traveled to Cleveland to return it.

CHRISTIAN ARCHIBALD HERTER (1865 - 1910), doctor and pathologist. He was a son of artist and interior designer Christian Herter, who designed the interiors of J. P. Morgan's home as well as several Vanderbilt homes. The son was Professor of Pharmacology and Therapeutics at the College of Physicians and Surgeons and is credited with helping to establish the study of biochemistry as a separate discipline in America. Herter was treasurer of the Rockefeller Institute for Medical Research (now Rockefeller University). An

Left: Lucy Carnegie, owner of much of Cumberland Island, accompanied her brother-in-law, Andrew Carnegie, to Jekyll in 1903. He was given a black tie dinner and is shown seated fourth from left next to Joseph Pulitzer. On Pulitzer's other side is Frederick G. Bourne. At far right is Myron Herrick, U. S. Ambassador to France, whose son was a Jekyll member.

accomplished cellist, he was a mentor of JIC member Lillie Bliss (daughter of JIC member Cornelius Bliss, Sr.), herself an excellent pianist, and solidified her lifelong interest in the arts. Through Herter she met Abby Aldrich Rockefeller, daughter of JIC member Nelson Aldrich, and they co-founded New York's Museum of Modern Art. In the months before her death, Lillie kept a photo of Herter (who died a year before her father) alongside those of her parents next to her bed. Herter married in 1886 Susan Dows, elder sister of JIC member Tracy Dows. Henry Drysdale Dakin, who worked in Herter's private laboratory in New York City from 1905 to 1914, was trained as an organic chemist in England. After Herter's untimely death in 1910 at the age of forty-five, Dakin continued directing Herter's laboratory at Mrs. Herter's request. In 1916, Dakin married Susan Dows Herter, and they moved to a house overlooking the Hudson River at Scarborough, where he constructed his own private laboratory in an annex. He discovered the enzymes arginase and glyoxidase and synthesized the hormone adrenalin. There is still a Susan Dows Herter Dakin Scholarship at the Manhattan School of Music.

ANDREW FOSTER HIGGINS (1831-1916), insurance executive. Born in Macon, Georgia, his father's financial reverses forced him to leave his studies at Columbia University. JIC member J. P. Morgan hired him to reorganize the U. S. division of Lloyds where he was able to return 2,000 percent on its stock. In 1907 he succeeded Charles T. Barney (who committed suicide over the bank's failure) as President of the Knickerbocker Trust Company. He formed with a partner the insurance firm of Johnson & Higgins which became the leading privately held insurance services and employee benefit consulting firm in the world. By 1997 the firm produced $1.2 billion in revenues and had 9,000 employees with 145 offices around the world. In that year, the firm was purchased by Marsh & McLennan in a merger valued at $1.8 billion. Higgins was a director of many corporations. He married Sarah H. Cornell and lived in Greenwich, Connecticut.

EUGENE HIGGINS (1858 - 1948), yachtsman. In 1898 a New York City newspaper account referred to Higgins as "not only the richest but the handsomest unmarried New Yorker." He inherited a fortune of $50 million from his father, Elias Higgins, who patented carpet-manufacturing devices with plants in New York City and Yonkers. The son, who won the American fencing championship in 1890, had a home on Fifth Avenue that was called "a mecca of high society" as well as a country home in Morristown, New Jersey. Many women were rumored to be engaged to him, including the opera singer Emma Calve in 1906 but he never married. During the spring and summer of 1900, Higgins welcomed King Christian of Denmark, Grand Duke Alexis of Russia, and Kaiser Wilhelm II of Germany aboard the steam yacht *Varuna*, which was then the largest yacht flying the flag of the New York Yacht Club. In 1908 the *Varuna*, during its twenty-sixth trans-Atlantic crossing, went ashore in the Madeira Islands and he was credited with saving the lives of his guests (including a count). The owner, the three ladies accompanying him, the captain and other officers and crew, totaling about fifty, were saved but one sailor was lost. Many crewmembers were in the water for nine hours before being rescued by a passing

Top: The wreck of the Varuna. One sailor's life was lost and many of its fifty crew members were in the water for hours before being rescued by a passing steamer.

Bottom: Andrew F. Higgins who founded an insurance business now valued at more than one billion dollars.

steamer. There is a four-foot model of the *Varuna* on display at Mystic Seaport. It is said that, when the *Varuna's* captain later wrote to Higgins asking him for a reference, Higgins returned the letter with only a photograph of the wrecked yacht. He died in England at his hotel suite at Torquay, Devon, where he lived for the last nine years of his life, although he still kept homes in Paris and New York City. His will gave $40 million to Columbia, Yale, Harvard, and Princeton for science education. All Higgins' employees, including his house staff, received substantial legacies, as did his nieces and nephews. He also left $100,000 to build his mausoleum in Woodlawn Cemetery. His will included a bequest to his second cousin, Gladys Deacon, second wife of the 9th Duke of Marlborough, whose first wife was Consuelo, daughter of JIC member William K. Vanderbilt. Gladys married the Duke at Higgins' Paris home where her mother was reportedly scandalized by the prominent paintings of nudes lining the walls.

JAMES JEROME HILL (1838 - 1916), railroad president. James J. Hill was born in Ontario and moved to St. Paul in 1856, where he first worked as a shipping clerk for J. W. Bass and Company. Between 1866 and 1879 he prospered in a series of wood, coal, and transportation partnerships. He was general manager (1879-1881), vice president (1881-1882), and president (1882-1890) of the St. Paul, Minneapolis and Manitoba Railway Company. In 1890 the railroad became the Great Northern Railway Company, with Hill as president (1890-1907) and later chairman of the board (1907-1912). He organized and owned the Great Northern Railway, having over 8,300 miles of mainline track at the time of his death. Hill was known as the "empire builder" and eventually, along with his ally, JIC member J. P. Morgan, controlled the ownership of Great Northern's largest competitor, the Northern Pacific, as well as the Chicago, Burlington & Quincy and the Spokane, Portland & Seattle Rail lines. Beginning in 1894, Hill organized three separate steamship companies with vessels that first operated on the Great Lakes and later on the Pacific Ocean. Hill played a major role in planning and constructing the Canadian Pacific Railroad and was an advisor to President Cleveland. In 1867 he married Mary Theresa, daughter of Timothy Mehegan of St. Paul. He gave $500,000 to build and endow a St. Paul seminary to prepare Catholic priests. Five of his sons-in-laws were JIC members: Erasmus C. Lindley, George T. Slade, Anson McCook Beard, Egil Boeckmann, and Michael Gavin, as well as his widow and his daughter, Ruth. In 1887 he commissioned the architectural firm of Peabody and Sterns of Boston to build the magnificent mansion at 240 Summit Avenue, St. Paul. It was in the great gallery of this house that he installed his most famous paintings, including more than two dozen by Corot. During the early decades of the twentieth century, Hill and five of his nine children had homes within a few blocks of each other, all on Summit Avenue. Hill and a number of his children also maintained permanent homes in New York City and the surrounding area.

MARY THERESA MEHEGAN HILL (Mrs. James Jerome Hill) (1846-1921). Born in New York City, she moved to St. Paul in 1850 and completed her education at a convent, Saint Mary's Institute, in Milwaukee. She married James J. Hill in 1867. At

his death she inherited $16.5 million and, although she continued her charities, she left an estate of $15 million. Mary Hill was long active in St. Paul's Catholic community and financially supported many of its institutions and causes. Her children were Mary Francis "Mamie" (Mrs. Samuel Hill), James Norman, Louis Warren, Clara (Mrs. Erasmus C. Lindley), Charlotte Elizabeth (Mrs. George T. Slade), Ruth (Mrs. Anson McCook Beard, then Mrs. Pierre Lorillard, then Mrs. Emile John Heidsieck), Rachel (Mrs. Egil Boeckmann), Gertrude (Mrs. Michael Gavin), and Walter Jerome. A daughter, Katie, died in infancy (1876). After her husband's death, she became a JIC member in her own right and remained one until her own death.

MARY ELIOT BETTS HOADLEY (Mrs. Russell H. Hoadley) (1871 - 1949). A daughter of Frederic H. and Louise Holbrook Betts, she was the widow of a prominent real estate broker. She served as volunteer organist at the Episcopal Church of St. Andrews by the Dunes in Southampton, Long Island, and had a summer home, "Mocomanto," at Southampton. Her son, Sheldon, was killed in World War I; her daughters were Mrs. Ellery James and Mrs. Lydig Hoyt. She became a JIC member in her own right in 1926 and remained one until 1930.

Top: Mrs. James J. Hill, a Jekyll widow and member in her own right, surrounded by her daughters, clockwise from left: Rachel, Clara, Gertrude, Charlotte, Ruth (who also became a Jekyll member), and Mary.

Bottom: The Hills' art-filled home in St. Paul. Five of his nine children had homes within walking distance of his own.

CHARLES FREDERICK HOFFMAN (1830 - 1897), priest and philanthropist. The Rev. Dr. Charles F. Hoffman, rector and builder of All Angels Episcopal Church in New York City, was a nephew of JIC member The Very Rev. Dr. Eugene A. Hoffman, dean of the General Theological Seminary for many years and father of JIC member William M. V. Hoffman. He became rector of St. Philips in the Highlands Episcopal Church in Garrison, New York, in 1860, and was largely responsible for the church's expansion after the arrival of the Hudson River Railroad fifteen years earlier that brought many new families to Garrison, including the Fishes, the Sloans, and the Pierponts. Hoffman led the drive to build a new Victorian gothic granite church designed by the same architect who was responsible for the new Trinity Church building in New York City. Hamilton Fish, then a United States Senator and later the Governor of New York, was elected to the vestry and would continue to serve until his death in 1893. (The current rector of St. Philips in the Highlands is a great-grandson of JIC member Helen Hartley Jenkins.) Charles F. Hoffman married Eleanor Louisa Vail, who was a prominent member of New York Society where she was listed in Mrs. Astor's "400." He provided the construction cost for the library named in his honor at the Medical University of South Carolina and was instrumental in the founding of Bard College (to which he gave more than $300,000) and served as a trustee. Hoffman was also a great promoter of the University of the South at Sewanee, Tennessee. In 1896 before leaving the University, he expressed his concern for the need of a dormitory and desired to donate part of the money to build it. Before the papers could

be drafted, Hoffman died at Jekyll Island on March 4, 1897. His heirs, wanting to fulfill his wishes, donated the Hoffman home to the University of the South, to be dismantled and moved to the University for a dormitory. In 1898, when the University proceeded to dismantle the Hoffman House at Bridgeport, an injunction was filed by the Bridgeport Land and Improvement Company. After delay and much expense the injunction was dissolved. It required eighty-two heavily loaded railroad cars to transport the Hoffman House to Sewanee, Tennessee. Every piece of the house was brought to Sewanee and was used either in the Hoffman Memorial Hall or in the five smaller structures that were erected. Hoffman Memorial Hall was destroyed by fire in 1919. The Hoffmans had a daughter, Mrs. J. Van Vechten Olcott, and two sons, Charles F., Jr. and JIC member William M. Vail Hoffman. The elder son, Charles, Jr., married in 1900 Zelia K. Preston, whose father was president of the Hibernia National Bank in New Orleans and a close advisor of President Cleveland. After her husband's death, Zelia moved to England and occupied several historic homes. In 1925 she purchased Burleigh House at King's Lynn in Norfolk and in 1928 became a British subject. The next year she ran for Parliament but lost.

EUGENE AUGUSTUS HOFFMAN (1829 – 1902), priest and seminary dean. The Very Rev. Dr. Hoffman was the uncle of JIC member, the Rev. Dr. Charles Frederick Hoffman. An Episcopal priest, he held several doctorates of divinity from U. S. and English universities and was dean of the General Theological Seminary from 1879 to 1902. His gifts to the seminary, including a Gutenberg

Bible, surpassed $1 million. In 1852 Hoffman married Mary Crooke Elmendorf. He was president of the New York Historical Society and died on a train returning to New York City from Canada. His first Hoffman ancestor, Martinus Hoffman, emigrated to the U. S. from Sweden in 1657.

WILLIAM MITCHELL VAIL HOFFMAN (1863-1947), estate executor. A son of JIC member the Rev. Dr. Charles Frederick Hoffman, his wife was a sister of Mrs. Stuart Duncan, whose husband was a JIC member. He was president of the Hoffman Estate and, with his brother, Charles F., Jr., was a partner in Hoffman Brothers, a real estate company. He served as trustee of the estate of his great-uncle, JIC member Eugene A. Hoffman, and as a trustee of St. Luke's Hospital, the Cathedral of St. John the Divine, and of Hobart College. They had two sons, Charles Gouverneur Hoffman, who was an amateur poet, and William, Jr., a priest and missionary who served in Japan and pre-deceased his father in 1944. They lived in Manhattan and at Tuxedo Park. Hoffman was fond of trotting horses and drove a four-in-hand.

EDWIN OLAF HOLTER (1871- 1964), social activist. Holter graduated from Yale and Columbia law school and served in the Spanish American War. He was president of the Prison Association of New York 1927-1954, which was concerned with the introduction and improvement of correctional techniques. He was a trustee of the Scandinavian-American Foundation. Holter's wife was a member of the Sage family and they had a son, Edwin, Jr., and two daughters, Mrs. Philip Ives and Mrs. Carlo Vicario.

ELON HUNTINGTON HOOKER (1869 -1938), civil engineer and manufacturing chemist. He was founder and president of the Hooker Electrochemical Company, said to be the largest electrolytic producer of chemicals in the U.S. Hooker was president of the Manufacturing Chemists Association of America, a close friend of President Theodore Roosevelt, and National Treasurer of the Progressive Party. In 1899 Roosevelt appointed him deputy superintendent of public works for the State of New York. In 1920 he was a candidate for the Republican nomination for governor of New York but was not successful. In 1901 Hooker married Blanche Ferry and they lived at Park Avenue. One of their daughters, Blanchette, married John D. Rockefeller III. The Hookers' grandson is current U. S. Senator John D. Rockefeller IV. Hooker died at the Hotel Huntington in Pasadena, but left no will with an estate of more than $600,000. His widow died in 1956, having been a benefactor of the New York Botanical Garden. She was president of the Vassar class of 1894 and, with her sister, gave Vassar its campus Alumnae House.

WALTER EWING HOPE (1879 -1948), attorney. Hope was a partner at Milbank, Tweed, & Hope as well as a director of corporations. He was appointed by President Hoover assistant secretary of the U. S. Treasury in 1929 and served as chairman of the National Republican Finance Committee. Hope was chairman of the Executive Committee of Princeton University.

AMOS LAWRENCE HOPKINS (1844 - 1912), railroad president. "Lawrie" Hopkins was a son of the president of Williams College. He left his studies to serve in the Union Army and was wounded at the Battle of the Wilderness. He entered the railroad

Top: The Elon H. Hooker home in Greenwich, Connecticut.

Bottom: Elon H. Hooker, father-in-law of John D. Rockefeller, III and grandfather of Senator Jay Rockefeller, IV.

business with the Housatonic in Bridgeport, Connecticut, then became Vice President of the Illinois Central. He married in 1871 but his wife and their infant daughter died less than two years later. When he was an officer with the Wabash, St. Louis, and Pacific, he became a friend and ally of Jay Gould. Hopkins married in 1879 Minnie Dunlap, daughter of the director of the Chicago Board of Trade, and they moved next door to the Goulds in New York City. Within several years the Hopkins marriage was the subject of gossip and, at their 1885 divorce, Flora Payne Whitney, wife of the U. S. Secretary of the Navy, testified on behalf of Mrs. Hopkins. He then returned to Williamstown and began acquiring land to establish a farm. In 1889 Hopkins retired from the Gould railroad enterprises (some said he was forced out by Gould's eldest son, JIC member George Jay Gould) and concentrated on expanding his extensive landholdings. In 1892 he married Maria Theresa Burnham Dodge and re-entered the railroad business. Hopkins eventually became president of the New York, Susquehanna & Western Railroad Company as well as receiver for the Chicago & Northern Pacific Railroad Company. Hopkins' widow gave more than twenty-five hundred acres of land to Williams College, still known as the Amos Lawrence Hopkins Memorial Forest.

BAYARD CUSHING HOPPIN (1884- 1956), broker. He and his brother, JIC member Gerard Beekman Hoppin, were the sons of William W. and Katherine Beekman Hoppin. They were the founders of Hoppin Brothers, members of the New York Stock Exchange. He graduated from Yale and was a director of the Beekman estate. Hoppin married Helen Alexandre in 1910 and, after their divorce, he married Laurette Kennedy. The Hoppins' sisters were Katharine Post and Esther Pool.

GERARD BEEKMAN HOPPIN (1869 -1950), broker. His grandfather was governor of Rhode Island. Hoppin graduated from Yale, served in the Spanish-American War and was decorated for his service in France in World War I. A partner with his much younger brother, JIC member Bayard Cushing Hoppin, at Hoppin Brothers & Company, stock brokers, he was also an incorporator of the Beekman Estate. He was president of the Metropolitan Opera Real Estate Company until 1940 when the Opera House was sold to the Metropolitan Opera Association. In 1924 he married Rosina Sherman, daughter of Alfred Miller Hoyt and a great-niece of Gen. William Sherman. They lived at "Four Winds," his estate at Oyster Bay Cove, Long Island, and had no children.

ALANSON BIGELOW HOUGHTON (1863 - 1941), manufacturer and diplomat. A son of Amory Houghton, Jr., his grandfather founded the glassmaking plant at Corning, New York, as the Corning Glass Works. In 1910 Alanson Houghton became president of Corning Glass Works at his father's death and from 1919 to 1928 was chairman of the board, continuing from 1929 until his death as chairman of the executive committee. He was elected to Congress 1918-22 and resigned his seat when President Harding appointed him our first ambassador to Germany after the close of World War I, where he served, 1922-25. In 1925 he was given the highest U.S. diplomatic post as ambassador to the Court of St. James and remained there for four years. Houghton was the Republican nominee for U. S. Senate from New York in 1928 but was defeated. He served as a trustee of the Brookings Institution and treasurer of the Carnegie Endowment for International Peace. In 1891 he married Adelaide Wellington. Although a highly successful diplomat, the *New York Times* referred to him in his obituary as "suavity personified. He seemed never to be in a hurry." His will included property at Jekyll Island left to his widow. They lived at "The Knoll" in Corning, New York, and had a summer home in South Dartmouth, Massachusetts.

HENRY ELIAS HOWLAND (1835 - 1913), attorney and judge. A Yale graduate, in 1865 he married Louise Miller. She died in 1884 leaving three children, and ten years later he married Mrs. Thomas B. Curtis of Boston. Howland and Chauncey Depew were considered the two finest after-dinner speakers in New York City. He coined the phrase, "The best thing out of Boston is the five o'clock train." Howland served as president of the University Club and also the Yale Club.

ELIJAH KENT HUBBARD (1835 - 1915), manufacturer. Hubbard was one of the first white children born in Chicago only one year after his parents' move from Connecticut. He succeeded his uncle as president of the Russell Manufacturing Company of Middletown, Connecticut. In 1864 Hubbard married Anna, daughter of Elisha Dyer, governor of Rhode Island. They had three sons and two daughters and she died in 1884. In 1897 he married Margaret, daughter of Henry G. Hubbard.

THOMAS HAMLIN HUBBARD (1838 -1915), attorney. Son of a governor of Maine, Hubbard served as a general in the Civil War. A partner at the New York law firm of Barney, Butler and Parsons, he was a lawyer for many railroads and declined the presidency of the Southern Pacific Railroad. Hubbard managed the estate of Mark Hopkins, for which he received $75,000 per year. He was also executor of the estate of Collis P. Huntington. He was president of the Peary Arctic Club, which helped finance Admiral Peary's journey to the North Pole. One of Peary's first actions upon his return was to travel to Portland, Maine, to place in General Hubbard's hands the proof of his having reached the Pole (Peary named Cape Thomas H. Hubbard in his honor). Hubbard gave a building to Bowdoin College, his alma mater, and endowed a chair at Albany Law School. He married in 1868 Sibyl A. Fahnestock, sister of Harris C. Fahnestock, a former partner of Jay Cooke and vice president of the First National Bank of New York. They had a son and two daughters and lived in Manhattan and at "Hillcrest" in Bar Harbour, Maine. One of Hubbard's pallbearers was Admiral Peary.

CHARLES LIVINGSTON HYDE (1863-1925), banker and railroad president. Hyde was an 1886 graduate of Yale. He was vice president of the New Orleans and Northwestern Railroad and president of the Brunswick and Birmingham Railroads. His first wife, a daughter of Charles Godfrey, died in 1904. Three years later he married Kathlyn Berrien Stryker, daughter of General William Scudder Stryker. Their daughter was Dorothy, Mrs. Darragh A. Park of Westbury, Long Island, and their son was Louis K. Hyde. He died in Plainfield, New Jersey.

HENRY BALDWIN HYDE (1834 -1899), insurance executive. In 1859 he founded the Equitable Life Assurance Company, the largest insurance company in the world at his death. He was born

Above: The Hubbard Free Library in Hallowell, Maine, was a gift of Thomas H. Hubbard, who helped finance Admiral Peary's North Pole expedition. Peary was one of Hubbard's pall bearers.

Left: Alanson Houghton, the first U. S. Ambassador to Germany after World War I and later Ambassador to Great Britain.

Right: Henry Howland, who quipped, "The best thing out of Boston is the five o'clock train."

in Catskill, New York, where his father, Henry Hazen Hyde, was actively engaged in mercantile business. As a young man he secured a mercantile clerkship in New York City and remained there for two years. In 1852 he was given an entry-level position in the Mutual Life Insurance Company at the same time his father was appointed an agent of the company. He learned the business and decided to strike out on his own in 1859, raising $100,000 in capital and renting office space for his new business on the floor above the Mutual's headquarters. Hyde established himself as a member of the Fifth Avenue Presbyterian Church where he met many of the financial figures who would figure prominently in his success. The minister's son, James W. Alexander, served in Hyde's wedding and his family became intimately involved in running the Equitable. Hyde built a luxurious corporate headquarters at 120 Broadway. Beginning in 1895, Hyde became so integral to the operation of the JIC that his son dubbed him "the Czar of Jekyll Island." He led the efforts to build "Sans Souci" at the Club, the nation's first condominium. Hyde married in 1864 Annie Fitch. Their children were Mary, who married Sidney Dillon Ripley, a grandson of the president of the Union Pacific Railroad; and James Hazen (called "Caleb" by his family), who was handed control of the firm at his father's death at much too young an age. The son was constantly mentioned in society coverage and was famed as a coachman. James was the second husband of Marthe Leishman (her first had been Count Louis de Gontaut-Biron), whose father was John G. A. Leishman, U. S. Ambassador to Germany and former president of Carnegie Steel Company. Marthe was given in marriage by her brother-in-law, the Duke of Croy, who was

Son of the "Czar of Jekyll Island," James Hazen Hyde was a celebrated coachman and dashing figure on the social scene until his infamous 1905 Ball in New York City. He was falsely accused of having charged it to his company but lost control when those who were older and more manipulative took advantage of his youth and inexperience.

married to Marthe's sister, Nancy. James' next wife was Helena "Ella" Holbrook Walker, heiress to the Hiram Walker distillery, whose first husband had been Manfred, Count Matushcka, Baron von Toppolczan and Apaetgen (Ella's next husband was Prince Alexander von Thurn & Taxis, 1st Prince della Torre e Tasso, 1st Duca di Castel Duino). James' final wife was French widow Marthe Dervaux Thom.   Two Hyde grandchildren displayed some of their grandfather's determination. Annah Ripley married Count Pierre de Vielcastel and secretly smuggled intelligence on notes hidden in egg baskets to nearby villagers in Normandy when the Germans occupied her home during World War II. Grandson Henry Hyde was an active agent for the O.S.S., forerunner of the C.I.A., in Algiers, employing his linguistic abilities to their best use in gathering information for the Allies. In 1905 James Hazen Hyde gave a highly-publicized costume ball in New York City featuring the French actress Rejane. The $200,000 spent on the evening was falsely attributed to having been paid by the Equitable in a smear campaign employed by E. H. Harriman, JIC member J. P. Morgan, and company president James W. Alexander, who had been such a close friend and advisor to the senior Hyde.   The son lost control of the company and retreated to France, where he remained a dashing figure on the social scene as well as an inveterate book collector and Francophile. The Equitable was sold to the French financial giant AXA and renamed in 2004 AXA Equitable Life Insurance Company.

JOHN HAMILTON INMAN (1844 - 1896), merchant and financier. Inman left school while young out of financial necessity.

After serving in the Confederate Army, he moved to New York City because his home and business had been destroyed. With only $100, he became a clerk in a cotton house. Three years later he established his own business of Inman, Swann & Company, credited with making New York the cotton capital of the U.S by founding the New York Cotton Exchange. Inman became known as the "Cotton King," made a sizeable fortune and took his new-found capital to the South. Determined to develop southern resources, he and other capitalists who relied upon him invested over $5 million in organizing the Tennessee coal, iron, and railroad company, including the bituminous coal-mines at Birmingham, Alabama, its blast-furnaces, and the Bessemer steel works nearby. He induced the investment of over $100 million in southern enterprises and became a director in companies that possessed more than ten thousand miles of railroad. He was also a director of the Louisiana and Nashville Railroad Company. In 1870 he married Margaret, daughter of James A. Coffin and granddaughter of the president of Greenville College. The town of Inman, South Carolina, served by the Southern Railway on whose board he served, was named in his honor.

WILLIAM BRADLEY ISHAM (1827 – 1909), leather merchant. He and his brother, Charles, were leather merchants from Malden, New York, who moved their business to New York City. He became Vice President of the Union Bank and of the Bank of the Metropolis. Isham retired from business in 1890 and sent the only Manhattan-grown wheat to the Columbia Exposition and to the Chicago World's Fair in 1893. In 1864 he purchased twenty-four acres along what is now Broadway, from 211th Street to 214th Street and there built his own mansion on its highest point. In 1911 his daughter, Julia, gave the family home there to New York City for use as a park, and the gift was enlarged in 1912, 1915, and 1917. The property originally included the Isham mansion, stables, and green house, with the main home located at the summit of the hill. These structures were demolished in the 1940s because of prohibitive maintenance costs. Isham was a major benefactor of Mount Washington Presbyterian Church. In 1852 he married Julia Burhans, and among their children were William Burhans (who left $1 million and his residence to Princeton) and Samuel, who was a well-known painter. His daughter-in-law, Hannah Collins Isham, died in 1948 at Vernon Hall on Long Island, which she had leased from the American-born Princess Irbain-Khan Kaplanoff. A marble jardiniere by Auguste Rodin, made to order for William Isham's artist son, Samuel, was given to the Museum of Fine Arts in Boston by William's daughter, Julia Isham Taylor, wife of the historian and author, Henry Osborn Taylor.

HENRY AMMON JAMES (1854 – 1929), attorney. Born in Baltimore, he graduated from Yale in 1874 and Yale law school in 1878. He began practicing law in New York City in 1888 and published a book, *Communism in America,* which was the winner of the John Porter Prize Essay at Yale. His daughter, Augusta, was the wife of JIC member Allan McClane.

LUCY WORTHAM JAMES (Mrs. Huntington Wilson) (1882-1938). Born in St. Louis, she was the great-granddaughter of Thomas James, founder of Maramec Iron Works, the first successful ironworks west of the Mississippi River. Her grandmother's brother was Robert Graham Dun, one of the country's pioneers in credit reporting and financial information. The firm he founded later became the Dun & Bradstreet Corporation (at the time, Dun's income reportedly exceeded $1,000 per day). After her mother's death from tuberculosis when Lucy was fourteen, she moved to New York City to live with her great-uncle, R.G. Dun, and his wife, Mary Bradford Dun, at their mansion on Madison Avenue for six years, until R.G. Dun passed away in November, 1900, leaving her a very wealthy young woman. Lucy then moved to Vienna, Austria, to study piano under the Polish pianist and composer Theodore Leschetizky. In 1904, Lucy Wortham James married Huntington Wilson, whom she met the year before while visiting relatives in Japan. He served as assistant secretary of state under William Jennings Bryan. After their wedding in Baltimore, the newlyweds returned to Japan where Huntington became the first secretary of the American Legation. At their home, Lucy and Huntington entertained many guests, including Captain John Pershing, Jack London, Mr. and Mrs. E.H. Harriman, and William Howard Taft. When they returned to Washington in 1912, Huntington and Lucy campaigned for President Taft during his re-election campaign. Taft lost the election and Huntington resigned from the state department. Lucy and Huntington then went on a tour of Central and South America. While in the Andes, Lucy suffered a severe attack of altitude sickness. Returning home, she was treated at John Hopkins University Hospital. From that time until her death, she never fully regained her health. The principles of protocol

within the U. S. State Department were said to be founded partially on Huntington Wilson's insistence that they be based "simply on the crude principles of ordinary kindness." In 1945 he wrote his autobiography, *Memoirs of an Ex-Diplomat.* Huntington and Lucy had no children and divorced in 1915. From that point, she always called herself "Mrs. Lucy Wortham James." In 1924 she gave $400,000 for the establishment of a women's clinic at Johns Hopkins Hospital. She established the James Foundation to operate in perpetuity Maramenec Springs Park in Missouri.

NORMAN JAMES (JIC member 1918-1931), book collector. A Baltimore native, he was a son of Henry and Amelia James of Baltimore and a brother of JIC member Walter B. James. He was a book collector of natural history and Americana and, in 1946, a selection of sixty-eight Audubon bird prints from his collection and those of his brother were displayed at the National Gallery of Art in Washington, D.C. He married Isabella (Belle) Hagner (1876-1943), the first salaried social secretary to a first lady (Edith Roosevelt, Helen Taft, and Ellen Wilson). After Mrs. Wilson's death she continued to plan White House social functions for the president until his remarriage in 1915. She planned Alice Roosevelt's debut (1902) and wedding (1906), and the weddings of Jessie Wilson (1913) and Eleanor Wilson (1914). Her extensive collection of papers, including autographed photographs from presidential families, is now in the White House. A feature story about her appeared in the *New York Times* in 1923 headlined, "The First Lady's Right-Hand Woman." She died in 1943.

Top left: Lucy Wortham James, whose early tutelage under her great-uncle, Robert G. Dun, as well as the fortune he left her, were appropriate training for the wife of a diplomat.

Top right: Dr. Walter B. James, one of the Jekyll Island Club's most beloved presidents, who was related by blood or marriage to many of its members.

Bottom: Dr. Walter B. James on the Jekyll golf course with the golf-loving William Lawrence, Episcopal Bishop of Massachusetts.

Philanthropist Helen Hartley Jenkins served as a surrogate mother-in-law to Geraldine Rockefeller Dodge.

WALTER BELKNAP JAMES (1858 - 1927), physician. An 1879 graduate of Yale, he began his practice in New York City in 1886 after medical studies in the U. S. and abroad. James served as a trustee of Columbia University and the American Museum of Natural History. In 1894 he married Helen Goodsell Jennings, niece of JIC member William Rockefeller and daughter of Oliver Burr Jennings. Her sisters, Annie Burr Jennings and Emma Burr Jennings Auchincloss, and her brother, Walter Jennings, were JIC members. Walter James' son, Oliver B. James, married a daughter of JIC member Alvin W. Krech, while his daughter, Eunice, married JIC member Henry E. Coe. He served as president of the New York Academy of Medicine from 1915 till 1918 when he suffered an eye hemorrhage and was unable to continue practicing medicine. He became active in philanthropies and on many boards and was elected president of the Jekyll Island Club in 1919, serving in that capacity until his death. He purchased Cherokee Cottage at Jekyll from the parents-in-law of Edwin Gould. James became ill at Jekyll Island and had just returned to his New York City home when he died. He lived at "Eagle's Beak," in Cold Spring Harbor on Long Island and was the most beloved president of the Jekyll Island Club. A brick wall surrounding the Club's swimming pool was erected and named in his honor.

HELEN GOODSELL JENNINGS JAMES (Mrs. Walter B. James) (JIC member 1926-1942; died 1946). A niece of JIC member William Rockefeller, she was the sister of JIC members Annie Burr Jennings, Emma Burr Jennings Auchincloss, and Walter Jennings. She was elected a member in her own right in 1926 and remained one until 1942, four years before her death. In her declining years the family of her sister, Mrs. Hugh D. Auchincloss, used her Jekyll home, Cherokee Cottage.

JAMES NEWBEGIN JARVIE (1853 - 1929), financier. Born in England, Jarvie came to America as a boy and began working at Arbuckle Brothers of New York City, importers of sugar, tea and coffee. He eventually became a partner and was so successful that he became known as "the Coffee King." Jarvie retired in 1906 and managed his many corporate directorships. He gave to Bloomfield, New Jersey, the Jarvie Memorial Library and in New York City established the Jarvie Commonweal Fund for Aged Persons, which still exists. A director of the Juilliard School, he also bequeathed $3 million to the Presbyterian Church and $250,000 to their foreign missions. In 1909 he married Helen Newton, and she was killed in 1917 in a yacht explosion at New London, Connecticut. Jarvie died on board the *Homeric* en route to Southampton, England, with his three nephews for a golf holiday. He had lived at Montclair, New Jersey, and had no children.

HELEN HARTLEY JENKINS (Mrs. George Walker Jenkins) (1860 - 1934), philanthropist. Her father, Marcellus Hartley, founded the Union Metallic Cartridge Company which combined with the Remington Arms Company. She endowed the founding of the School of Nursing at Columbia University, from which her nephew, Marcellus Hartley Dodge, graduated in 1903. Her extensive philanthropies centered upon nursing but included many others. She gave the Grace Hospital in Banner Elk, North Carolina, in memory of her twin sister. Jenkins was president of the Hartley Corporation of Hartford, Connecticut, which she founded for philanthropic purposes. She established Hartley Farms in New Jersey as a refuge for underprivileged children and adults to visit during the summer. Barnard College, her daughter's alma mater, was another of her favorite beneficiaries. Her home in Morristown, New Jersey, was destroyed by fire in 1930 and she had to be carried to safety. She married in 1894 George Walker Jenkins, president of the American Deposit and Loan Company, and they had two daughters. The physical fitness center at Columbia University is named for Marcellus Hartley Dodge, the nephew whom she treated as a son (his mother died in childbirth), and who married a daughter of JIC member William Rockefeller. Jenkins purchased Indian Mound, Rockefeller's Jekyll Island home, in 1924, complete with all its furnishings. At her death, she left it to her nephew who declined to accept the gift.

ANNIE BURR JENNINGS (1856- 1939), philanthropist. A daughter of Oliver Burr Jennings (1825-1893) and Esther Judson Goodsell Jennings, she lived at Park Avenue in New York City and at "Sunnie Holme" in Fairfield, Connecticut. Her father was an associate of both William and John D. Rockefeller and a vice president of Standard Oil, of which he owned ten percent of the total stock. Her father had been a California pioneer in 1849 and her mother was a sister of Mrs. William Rockefeller. Jennings was an active anti-suffragist. Her home in New York City was acquired in 1929 for the Union League Club. Along with her brother, Oliver Gould Jennings (1865-1936), and her sister, JIC member Emma Jennings Auchincloss, she was an active patron of Fairfield, Connecticut, and together they paid for the restoration of the

Morris K. Jesup, whose many philanthropies included the funding of Booker T. Washington's "movable schools" that operated from "Jesup wagons" carrying agricultural exhibits to rural areas. Even after they were mechanized the name remained "Jesup wagons" when their crew included a nurse as well as advisors who shared farming techniques.

Fairfield Town Hall. Her sister was married to JIC member Walter B. James. She funded the only extant garden in the U.S. designed by English gardener Gertrude Jekyll at Glebe House Museum in Woodbury, Connecticut. In 1928, after an introduction by the Grand Duchess Xenia (Mrs. William B. Leeds) she hosted at her home the woman who claimed to be the Grand Duchess Anastasia, murdered daughter of Russia's last tsar, Nicholas II, and continued to support her claims.

JEAN POLLOCK BROWN JENNINGS (Mrs. Walter Jennings) (1864 - 1949).   A daughter of Edward B. Brown of New York City, she married in 1891 Walter Jennings, vice president of Standard Oil. She was a horticulturalist and left bequests to the Cathedral of St. John the Divine as well as the Episcopal Church in Cold Spring Harbor. She lived and died at "Burrwood" in Cold Spring Harbor, and her children were Oliver B. Jennings, Mrs. Henry C. Taylor, and Mrs. Albert H. Ely. She assumed her husband's JIC membership share at his death and remained a member in her own right, finally deeding their Jekyll home, Villa Ospo, to the Club in 1942.

LAURA "LILA" HALL PARK JENNINGS (born 1858; JIC member 1920-24) (Mrs. Frederic Beach Jennings). She was a daughter of Trenor W. Park, who amassed a fortune in California overseeing the mining interests of John C. Fremont, and she was a granddaughter of Governor Hiland Hall of Vermont. Her husband (1853-1920), whom she married in 1880, was a lawyer and general counsel for the Associated Press and the Erie Railroad Company, as well as a corporate director. They lived at Park Avenue in New York City, and at "Fairview" in North Bennington, Vermont. JIC member

J. P. Morgan was one of her husband's pallbearers.

WALTER JENNINGS (1858 - 1933), oil executive. His father was one of the first directors of Standard Oil, the company for whom the son worked and was made a director in 1903. He practiced law for a short time with his relative, Frederic B. Jennings, whose wife was a JIC member. Walter Jennings was the brother of JIC members Helen Jennings James, Annie Burr Jennings, and Emma Jennings Auchincloss. His family's ownership of stock in Standard Oil was second only to those of the Rockefellers. Jennings was proud of his descent from U. S. Vice President Aaron Burr and named his estate on Long Island "Burrwood." He graduated from Yale and from Columbia Law School, where he was a classmate of Theodore Roosevelt. Jennings was president of the National Fuel Gas Company 1908-19 and collected American paintings. He died at Villa Ospo, his John Russell Pope-designed home on Jekyll Island, after his physician, Dr. Firor, was flown in from Johns Hopkins. Jennings' body was taken by private rail car to New York City on the Orange Blossom Special. His estate, "Burrwood," in Cold Spring Harbor, Long Island, was demolished in 1995.

MARIA VAN ANTWERP DEWITT JESUP (Mrs. Morris Ketchum Jesup) (1834 - 1914). She was a daughter of the Rev. Thomas DeWitt, pastor of the Dutch Collegiate Church in New York City. In 1854 she married Morris K. Jesup. At her husband's death in 1908 she inherited $9 million and continued his charities, especially to Presbyterian Hospital. She gave $150,000 to Yale and was a generous donor of her husband's art collection to the Metropolitan Museum of Art, the National Gallery, and other institutions.

MORRIS KETCHUM JESUP (1830 - 1908), financier and philanthropist. He was an organizer of Jesup, Kennedy & Company, dealers in railway supplies, along with JIC member John S. Kennedy, but retired in 1884 and remained as a special partner. Jesup was one of the founders of the YMCA and served as its president in 1872. Among his many philanthropies, he served as president of the American Museum of Natural History and gave it a collection of woods valued at more than $100,000 in 1881. He left the Museum $1 million in his will. He donated Jesup Hall to Union Theological Seminary and financed the Arctic expeditions of Admiral Robert Peary, who named for him Cape Morris K. Jesup at the northern end of Greenland. He and his wife, Maria DeWitt, lived in Manhattan; at Bar Harbour, Maine; and at "Belvoir Terrace" in Lenox, Massachusetts, designed by Rotch & Tilden and built between 1888-1890, with landscaping by Frederick Law Olmsted. Jesup gave the town library to Westport, Connecticut, where he was born. Jesup, Iowa, first settled about 1860, was named in his honor as he was president of the Dubuque and the Sioux City railroad that served it. Jesup was a major contributor to Booker T. Washington's work. Washington directed his faculty to "take their teaching into the community." George Washington Carver responded by designing a "movable school" that students built. The wagon was named for Jesup, who gave Washington the money to equip and operate the vehicle. The first was horse-drawn and called a Jesup Agricultural Wagon. Later it was a mechanized truck, still called a Jesup Wagon, that carried agricultural exhibits to county fairs and community gatherings. By 1930, the "Booker T. Washington Agricultural School on Wheels" carried a nurse, a home demonstration agent, an agricultural agent, and an architect to share the latest techniques with rural people.

AUGUSTINE DAVID LAWRENCE JEWETT (JIC member 1886-1898). He was a son of David Jewett (1772 – 1842), commander in the Brazilian Navy after his service in the U. S. Navy, and Mrs. Eliza McTiers, daughter of Augustine H. Lawrence, an alderman in New York City whom Jewett met while traveling to the U. S. on behalf of Brazil. He married in 1856 Elizabeth H. Dickisson and their son, Augustine D. L. Jewett II, was vice president of New York Trap Rock Corporation and died in 1954.

HUGO RICHARDS JOHNSTONE (JIC member 1899-1907), sportsman. He was a son-in-law of JIC member Samuel W. Allerton. Johnstone set a course record in 1910 at the Southern California Golf Association Tournament at Annandale. He was robbed of almost $9,000 worth of jewelry while playing golf at the Garden City Club in 1920. Johnstone married Kate Allerton and they lived at "Brackenside" in Hamilton, Massachusetts. She was a JIC member in her own right and died in 1937. Johnstone married secondly Alice Child who died in Coronado, California, in 1942, widow of John Purroy Mitchel, mayor of New York City from 1914 to 1917, who was the youngest person elected New York City mayor until that time. Mitchel had succeeded Mayor William Gaynor after he was assassinated, and in 1917 a gunman shot at Mayor Mitchel but hit his corporation counsel instead. Mitchel died when he fell out of an airplane during training exercises in Louisiana. Johnstone and his second wife lived in France before moving to California.

ALFRED WILLIAM JONES (JIC member 1946 - 1947), developer. With his cousin, Howard Coffin, founder of the Hudson Motor Car Company and United Airlines, he developed Sea Island, Georgia. Jones first came to the Georgia coast to recover from tuberculosis and, at the age of twenty-one, began to work with Coffin to develop Sea Island. Jones hired Addison Mizner as architect and built golf courses attracting the top international players. Sea Island is now run by his grandson, Alfred "Bill" Jones III, who brought international attention to Sea Island for hosting the G-8 summit in 2004. The Cloister was opened in 1928 with forty-six rooms and continues to be run by the Jones family. It was at the Jones' home on Sea Island that Winston Churchill's daughter, Sarah, wed Anthony Beauchamp in 1949. Jones continued the maintenance of Jekyll Island during the War years when it was closed and attempted to prevent its permanent demise.

NATHANIEL SCAMMON JONES (JIC member 1887-1891). Called by his middle name, he lived in Philadelphia. His sister, Countess de Benoist-d'Azy, was decorated for her volunteer work in France during World War I. He and his wife entertained the opera singer Nellie Melba when she visited Philadelphia in 1907.

FREDERIC AUGUSTUS KEEP (1855 -1911), lumber merchant. Keep was a Cleveland and Chicago lumberman who moved to Washington, D.C., in 1900. His wife, Florence, was a sister of Mabel Boardman, who succeeded her good friend Clara Barton as head of the U. S. Red Cross. Another sister was the wife of Massachusetts Governor and U. S. Senator W. Murray Crane, whose family owned the paper and stationery company. Keep died in Paris of appendicitis. His monument in Washington's Rock Creek Cemetery, featuring two semi-nude life-size figures, was designed by James Earle Fraser, who sculpted the famous American Indian statue, *The End of the Trail.* His wife lived until 1954 and is buried with her husband along with their infant son who died in 1902.

FREDERIC ROGERS KELLOGG (1867 -1935), attorney. He was a partner at Kellogg, Emery, and Inness-Brown and was the founder and first president of the National Community Chest of America. He married in 1903 Cornelia VanWyck Halsey and lived in Morristown, New Jersey. Their daughter, Cornelia, married Grinnell Morris, son of JIC member Ray Morris. The Kelloggs' son was the Rev. Frederic Brainerd Kellogg, Episcopal Chaplain at Harvard and Radcliffe from 1937 to 1958, who established the Kellogg lectureship in memory of his father. Upon the death of her son in 1958, Mrs. Frederic Rogers Kellogg continued the lectureship at Episcopal Divinity School as a memorial to her son and husband. She died in 1967.

EMMA BAKER KENNEDY (Mrs. John Stewart Kennedy) (1833 - 1930), philanthropist. Mrs. Kennedy was a daughter of Cornelius Baker. She founded the Hartford School of Missions and the Hartford School of Religious Pedagogy and gave endowments to both. She was a liberal contributor to Berea (Kentucky) College and Robert College (Constantinople), and built a theological seminary for the Waldensians in Rome, Italy. In 1911 the Hartford Seminary organized the Hartford School of Missions, incorporating in it the

John Stewart Kennedy, whose many contributions included building the United Charities Building in New York City. At his death, half of his $67 million estate went to charity.

missionary training that had long been growing within its own program. Mrs. Kennedy, a lifelong supporter of missionary work, endowed the school in memory of her husband and in his honor the name was changed to The Kennedy School of Missions. In 1918, she and Helen Miller Gould Shepard, sister of JIC members George Gould and Edwin Gould, became the first female vice presidents of the American Bible Society. The Kennedys had no children and were very close to the children of his sister, Mary Kennedy Tod.

JOHN STEWART KENNEDY (1830 - 1909), financier and philanthropist. Born in Scotland, he was a clerk in a local shipping company and was sent to the U. S. as their agent in 1850 for two years. Although he returned to Scotland to manage the company's Glasgow office, he was asked by JIC member Morris K. Jesup to come to the U. S. as his partner in Jesup and Company. In 1868 he established his own banking firm of J. S. Kennedy & Company and was later appointed by Congress as one of the incorporators of the Union Pacific Railroad. Kennedy became closely allied with JIC member James J. Hill in financing the Northwestern railway system, and a town on the line in Minnesota was named for him. In 1883 he retired and turned his business over to his sister's two sons, Robert E. Tod and John Kennedy Tod (for whom Tod's Point in Greenwich, Connecticut, is named). Kennedy then became a director of many corporations and railroads and concentrated on philanthropy. He was president of Presbyterian Hospital for the last twenty-five years

Van Rennsselaer Choate King, son of David H. King, Jr., was heavily decorated by the Belgian, French, and British governments for his services in World War I. His niece was the Duchess de la Rochefoucauld.

of his life and, on his golden wedding anniversary, he gave the hospital $1 million. He erected and paid for the United Charities Building to house non-profits in New York City and gave $500,000 to Columbia University and $250,000 to the School of Philanthropy. Kennedy was president of Lenox Library before its merger with New York Public Library (where his bust still adorns the lobby) and gave the Metropolitan Museum of Art the famous painting, *Washington Crossing the Delaware.* His will of $67 million left one-half of that amount to charity. Through the Kennedys' niece, Maria Howard Potter Tod, they were connected by marriage to JIC members and descendants Henry P. Davison, Fowler McCormick, James Alexander Stillman, Grace Goodyear Depew, and Cynthia Burke Roche, sister of JIC member Frank Burke-Roche and great-aunt of the late Diana, Princess of Wales.

MARSHALL RUTGERS KERNOCHAN (1880 -1955), composer. Kernochan studied music in the U. S. and in Germany. In 1931 he founded Galaxy Music Corporation, music publishers, in New York City, and served as its president until his death. Among his best-known compositions were "We Two Together," set to words by Whitman, and "Smuggler's Song," with words by Kipling. He married in Paris in 1918 Caroline Hatch, who served as a nurse in American hospitals in France during World War I. Kernochan was the grand marshal and grand treasurer of the Masons for the State of New York. He and his wife were active members of the Tuxedo Park colony. Their son, John, established Columbia University Law School's Kernochan Center for Law, Media and the Arts.

FRANKLIN MILLER KETCHUM (1838-1900), banker. He was a son of Morris Ketchum of Ketchum, Son & Company, one of the largest and most successful banking houses in New York City during and after the Civil War. His brother, Edward, bankrupted the family business by gold speculation, then attempted to forge checks to cover his tracks before escaping with the firm's remaining cash. He was caught and sentenced to prison at Sing Sing, where he was released in 1869 with time off for good behavior. Another brother, Landon Ketchum, was the father-in-law of Edwin Thorne, son of JIC member Samuel Thorne. Franklin M. Ketchum served as the first Treasurer of the Jekyll Island Club.

DAVID H. KING, JR. (1849 - 1916), contractor. King was the builder for the Washington Arch, the old Times Building of 1889 on Park Row, Stanford White's Madison Square Garden, and the base of the Statue of Liberty. He also built row houses and apartments called "Strivers Row," designed by McKim, Mead and White, at West 138th St. in 1890. At Jekyll Island he built for himself the only one-storey residence and one of the first in Georgia to have an in-ground swimming pool (it was later sold to Edwin Gould). Architect Stanford White was his guest at Jekyll in 1892. King and his family lived at Fifth Avenue and at Newport, Rhode Island. The Kings' granddaughter, Jeanne-Marie de Villiers du Terrage, first married Prince Martin Lubomirski (whose second wife was a granddaughter of JIC member Marshall Field) then married the 14th Duke de la Rochefoucauld, who survived her. The Kings' son, Van Rensselaer Choate King, was decorated in World War I by the British, French, and Belgium governments for having been responsible for all movements of freight and troops in Europe.

After the war he became superintendent of the Atlantic Coast Line Railroad.

HENRY WILLIAM KING (1828 - 1898), clothing manufacturer. King moved to Chicago from New York in 1854, entering business on South Water Street, and in 1868 he and W. C. Browning and other associates organized the wholesale clothing house of Henry W. King & Company. After the great fire the company moved to the wholesale clothing district around Market and Franklin streets. King became president of Browning, King & Company, the largest wholesale clothing firm in the U. S. He was also prominent in charitable work and was president of the Chicago Relief and Aid Society during the period of the great fire. In 1923 Browning King and Company established the first radio advertising when the Browning King Dance Orchestra went on the air. No direct advertising was permitted -- not even a mention of what Browning King's business was. But the company's name was attached to the orchestra which had been contracted to broadcast exclusively for Browning King, and no other firm. For the first time, entertainers and a sponsor were formally linked. The Kings' daughter, Elizabeth, married in 1888 Cyrus Bentley II, attorney for Chicago's McCormick family. H. W. King's wife, Aurelia, wrote a long personal account of the Chicago fire of 1871; she died in 1900.

OLIVER KANE KING (1836 - 1888), shipping merchant. He was a partner with JIC founding member Newton Finney as King, Finney & Company, railway bankers and shipping merchants in New York City. King helped Finney recruit appropriate members at the founding of the Jekyll Island Club. He served as a governor of New York City's Union Club where he was secretary 1869-1887. King died on his ranch in Garfield County, Colorado, and, according to his obituary in the *New York Times,* he was "the originator of the Restigouche Salmon Club and the Jekyll Island Club." Although one of the original incorporators, King's ill health forced him to resign his membership in the first year of the JIC's operation.

ALVIN WILLIAM KRECH (1858-1928), railroad executive and banker. Krech was secretary of the reorganization committee for the Union Pacific Railroad 1895-1906 and a director of several railroads. He was president of the Equitable Trust Company from 1903 until 1923 when he became chairman of the board. His daughter, Angeline, married Oliver B. James, son of JIC member Walter B. James. He died at his office desk in the Equitable Building, next door to J. P. Morgan & Company, which he was credited with building. He lived on Fifth Avenue and had a residence in Southampton. The governments of France, Italy, and Romania all decorated him for his work.

HENRY STEERS LAKE (JIC member 1912-1917). Lake was the son of George Graham Lake, who died while Henry was young. His grandfather, George Steers, designed the yacht *America,* that in 1851 brought the America's Cup racing trophy to the U. S. His mother, Frances Steers Lake, married JIC member Frederic Baker, who built "Solterra Cottage" at Jekyll. Lake and his wife lived on New York City's Central Park South. He died in Hollywood, California.

CHARLES LANIER (1837 - 1926), banker. He became a

partner in the banking firm of Winslow, Lanier & Company at age twenty-three and a senior member from 1860 for the remainder of his life. The firm was founded in New York in 1849 by his father, James F.D. Lanier, whose loans to the state of Indiana enabled the state to equip Union troops during the Civil War. His father left an estate of $10 million. The son was president of the Pittsburgh, Ft. Wayne & Chicago Railroad Company and a director of other corporations. Lanier was a close friend of JIC member J. P. Morgan and a part of his group, informally called the Corsair Club, which made its headquarters on Morgan's yacht. His wife was Sarah E. Egleston and they lived in New York City and at Lenox, Massachusetts. Mrs. William Averell Harriman was his niece. Lanier's father was a native of Madison, Indiana, where the Lanier Mansion remained in family hands until 1917, when Charles Lanier donated the property to the Jefferson County Historical Society and provided funds to enable that organization to operate it as the Lanier Memorial Museum. In 1925, the historical society turned the property over to the state of Indiana with the approval of the Lanier Family and it was opened to the public as Madison's first historic house museum.

LEONIDAS MOREAU LAWSON (1836 -1909), attorney and financier. Lawson graduated from the University of Missouri at the age of seventeen while serving as professor of Latin and Greek. He practiced law, served in the Missouri legislature, and was president of the St. Louis & St. Joseph Railroad. In 1868 he moved to New York City and became a partner in a banking firm before becoming the firm's resident partner in London 1874-78. He married in 1860

Charles Lanier, whose father's loans to the State of Indiana enabled the equipping of its Union soldiers during the Civil War. The son was a member of J. P. Morgan's "Corsair Group" that met on Morgan's yacht.

Theodosia Thornton and had sons Leonidas M., Jr., and JIC member William Thornton Lawson.

WILLIAM THORNTON LAWSON (born 1862; JIC member 1887-88), attorney. A son of JIC member Leonidas Moreau Lawson, he was an expert fencer. He graduated from Columbia in 1882 and in 1888 was the U. S. National Men's Foil Champion.

LEWIS CASS LEDYARD (1851-1932), attorney and yachtsman. Ledyard's father was the charge' d'affaires at the American legation at Paris. The son was a partner at the New York City law firm Carter, Ledyard & Milburn. He served as counsel for American Tobacco Company and helped reorganize it after the U.S. Supreme Court ordered its breakup. Ledyard was counsel for the U. S. Stock Exchange for thirty years. He succeeded his friend J. P. Morgan, whose personal attorney he was, as commandant of the New York Yacht Club. Ledyard was president of the New York Public Library to which he bequeathed $2 million. He was a trustee of the Metropolitan Museum of Art and of the Morgan Library and vice-president of the Frick Collection. Ledyard's niece, Matilda (daughter of Henry Brockholst Ledyard), was the Baroness Clemens August von Ketteler, whose husband, the German Ambassador in Peking, was murdered in 1900, triggering the Boxer Rebellion. Ledyard's grandson, Lewis III, married a daughter of JIC member Stanley G. Mortimer.

CORNELIUS SMITH LEE (JIC member 1919-1947), broker. "Connie" Lee's father was lost on the yacht *Cythera* in the West Indies in March of 1888, along with the father of JIC member William A. W. Stewart. Lee was a New York City stockbroker and an

The Corona, owned by attorney Lewis C. Ledyard, who succeeded client and friend J. P. Morgan as commandant of the New York Yacht Club.

All horses and livestock had to be ferried to Jekyll Island where private stables were in demand.

avid golfer who served as chairman of the JIC's greens committee. Lee lived in Tuxedo Park and in Edgartown, Massachusetts. His son, Cornelius, Jr., was owner of the H. P. Bissell Drug Company in Norwalk, Connecticut.

ELLIOT CABOT LEE (JIC member 1915-1920). He was a son of Boston banker Henry Lee and Elizabeth Perkins Cabot Lee, whose grandfather was the wealthiest man in New England, with a fortune derived from shipping trade with China. Elliot Cabot Lee, a brother of philanthropist Joseph Lee, was an 1876 graduate of Harvard. His sister, Elizabeth, was the wife of JIC member Frederick Cheever Shattuck. A sculpture of their mother by Horatio Greenough is in the Boston Atheneum.

JOHN THREADGOLD LESTER (1847 - 1890), merchant. He was a Chicago merchant whose business was Lester & Company. He married in 1863 Mary E. Shergold who died in 1876. From 1881 he had a home, "Blacktoft," at Lake Geneva and died in 1890 at the age of forty-three.

ERASMUS CHRISTOPHER LINDLEY (1870 -1957), attorney. He was vice president and general counsel of the Great Northern Railway. In 1922 Lindley resigned as an officer in the Great Northern but continued on the executive committee and as a director of the Northwestern Trust Company of St. Paul. Lindley married in 1917 Clara Ann Hill, a daughter of JIC member James J. Hill. They lived in St. Paul until her mother's death in 1921 when they moved to New York City. They also had a home in Tuxedo Park. Mrs. Lindley was active in Catholic charities and wrote an unfinished biography of her parents that her husband published privately in 1948.

CHARLES LONGSTRETH (1868 -1948), manufacturer and inventor. From 1886 to 1891 Longstreth worked for the Baldwin Locomotive Works owned by JIC member William L. Austin. In 1904 he became president of the U. S. Metallic Packing Company of Philadelphia, producer of railroad supplies. In 1891 he married Gertrude Heyer. Longstreth was a yachtsman and author on marine subjects. He died at his retirement home in Coronado, California.

EDWARD EUGENE LOOMIS (1864 -1937), railroad president. He was president of the Lehigh Valley Railroad Company and its subsidiaries, including the Lehigh Valley Coal Company, until late in life when he became chairman. Loomis was a director of several corporations, including AT&T. He was executor of the estate of Samuel Clemens and president of the Mark Twain Company. In 1902 he married Julia Langdon, a niece of Samuel Clemens. Their daughters were Mrs. Eugene Lada-Mocarski and Mrs. Bayard Schieffelin. He was particularly averse to publicity and, despite fifteen years of trying, journalists were never able to learn the exact date of Loomis' birth nor the details of his education. Ten years after succeeding as president of the Lehigh Valley Railroad, he was asked his opinions about American railways, and replied, "I'm not looking for publicity. I'm not into politics. I've no dull axes of any kind that need grinding." In a bitter 1928 fight for control of the Lehigh, Loomis won by only five thousand votes in a total of more than a million. He successfully carried the railroad through the Great Depression when others failed. He and his family lived at Holiday Farm in Murray Hill, New Jersey. His wife was an active benefactor of her alma mater, Bryn Mawr College, as well as St. Luke's Hospital.

JOHN MASON LOOMIS (1825 -1900), lumber merchant. Loomis married in 1849 Mary Hunt. He commanded a Union company during the Civil War when his wife accompanied him to the battle front and acted as the head of a company of Red Cross nurses. He purchased pinelands in Michigan, formed the Pere Marquette Lumber Company in 1878 and headed the company from Chicago. After he, his three brothers, and one sister had all lost all their children, he incorporated the Loomis Institute of Windsor Connecticut, to provide free education to all its citizens between the ages of twelve and twenty, and endowed it with $2 million. When his widow died in 1910 in Chicago, she had no heirs and her estate of $1.25 million was given to the Loomis Institute, now the Loomis Chaffee School, whose alumni include Ella Grasso, former governor of Connecticut; Henry Kravis, corporate financier and partner in Kohlberg Kravis Roberts & Company; John D. Rockefeller III, industrialist and philanthropist; Arthur Ochs Sulzberger, former publisher of *The New York Times;* and William Weld, former governor of Massachusetts.

PIERRE LORILLARD (1833 - 1901), sportsman and tobacco manufacturer. The fourth in line of the same name in his family, he was best-known as developer of the exclusive Tuxedo Park colony near New York City as well as the first American to win the English Derby. The first Pierre founded in 1760 the Lorillard Tobacco Company, the oldest and fourth-largest tobacco company in America. Its best-selling brand, Newport (named for the Rhode Island playground of the wealthy where the Lorillards owned the first Breakers and popularized yachting), is still the best-selling menthol cigarette in the U. S. The family of Pierre IV's mother, Catherine Griswold, owned the great New York mercantile house of N. L. & G. Griswold, known to their rivals as "No Loss and Great Gain Griswold," importers of rum, sugar, and tea. At the death of Pierre IV's grandfather in 1843, the term "millionaire" was first coined for his obituary. Diarist Philip Hone wrote at the time, "He was a tobacconist, and his memory will be preserved in the annals of New York by the celebrity of 'Lorillard's Snuff and Tobacco.' He led people by the nose for the best part of a century, and made his enormous fortune by giving them that to chew which they could not swallow." In 1858 he married Emily Taylor and they lived with their four children in a mansion at 8 Washington Square as well as at their homes in Newport and Tuxedo Park. He made a yachting capital of Newport where his schooner *Vesta* and steam yacht *Radha* were frequently berthed. His daughter, Maude, first married T. Suffern Tailer then Cecil Baring who succeeded as Baron Revelstoke after her death. Maude and her second husband were great patrons of the architect Edward Lutyens, who created their home at Lambay Island near Dubin. Their grandson is the current Baron. Lorillard's eldest son, Pierre V, married JIC member Ruth Hill Beard, daughter of JIC member James J. Hill, while his younger son, Griswold, is credited with having created the dinner jacket known as the "tuxedo," named for his father's creation of the exclusive retreat of the wealthy. One of Lorillard's nieces was

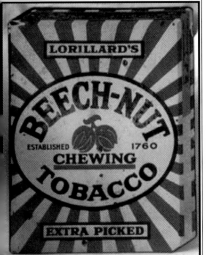

Top: Pierre Lorillard's home at Tuxedo Park, the exclusive colony he founded near New York City. He was also the first American to win the English Derby. His son, also named Pierre, married Jekyll member Ruth Hill Beard.

Bottom: When Lorillard's grandfather died, a diarist noted that he "made his enormous fortune by giving them that to chew which they could not swallow."

Edith Kip, who married a son of the 3rd Earl of Coventry, while still another was Helen Barbey who married the Count Hermann de Pourtales and was the first woman to compete in the Olympic games (sailing) representing her husband's home, Switzerland. Lorillard financed the expedition of the French archeologist Désiré Charnay and was awarded the French Legion of Honor for his contributions. Lorillard Avenue in the Bronx is named for him. He was estranged from his wife during their last years and left his extensive stables and farms at Rancocas Stable to his acknowledged mistress. His widow outlived him by twenty-four years.

RUTH HILL LORILLARD (Mrs. Anson McCook Beard, Mrs. Pierre Lorillard, Mrs. Emile John Heidsieck) (1879-1959). Her father was JIC member James J. Hill who developed the Great Northern Railroad. Her first husband, JIC member Anson McCook Beard, died in 1929, and in 1931 she married Pierre Lorillard V, son of JIC member Pierre Lorillard IV. His first wife had died in 1909 at their home in Washington. They lived at 820 Fifth Avenue and in Tuxedo Park, where both had homes before their marriage. After his death in 1940 she married a Frenchman, Emile John Heidsieck, whose family were prominent producers of Piper-Heidsieck champagne. Her children were Anson McCook Beard and Mary Hill Beard, who married Frederick C. Havemeyer.

GEORGE HENRY MACY (1858 -1918), tea merchant. President of Carter, Macy & Company of New York, Chicago, and San Francisco, and president of its overseas subsidiary, George H. Macy & Company. Carter, Macy had been founded by his father-in-law, Oliver S. Carter. Macy's own family firm had been Josiah

Macy & Son, tea merchants. He also served as a director of several corporations. His cousin was JIC member Valentine Everit Macy. He married Kate Louise Carter and among their children was JIC member William Kingsland Macy who married a daughter of JIC member John Henry Dick. One of George H. Macy's children was Helen who married Irving Kent Hall, a future partner at the family firm. Macy purchased in 1912 Jekyll's Moss Cottage from the estate of George Struthers. The Macys lived in Manhattan and at Islip, Long Island.

VALENTINE EVERIT MACY (1871 - 1930), estate executor. Everit was a son of Josiah Macy II (who merged his family's petroleum business with Standard Oil and became an officer there) and Caroline Everit Macy. His great-grandfather, Josiah Macy, was a sea captain and merchant who bought and settled Nantucket Island and moved to Westchester, New York, with his son, William, who later went into the petroleum business. Everit Macy served in the Wilson administration on the Council on Naval Defense and as an arbiter to the War Labor Board. He ran the family financial interests of his father, who died when Everit was five. In 1896 he married Edith W. Carpenter, and they had two sons and a daughter. Macy was president of the Westchester Park Commission and expanded Westchester County's parkland to seventeen thousand acres, including Rye Playland. When John D. Rockefeller offered $10 million to the Egyptian government to establish a museum in Cairo (later withdrawn), Macy was named as one of its three administrators. His wife, Edith, died in 1925. In her memory he gave a camp of three hundred acres near Briarcliff, New York, as

well as $100,000 for training its leaders. Macy lived at "Chilmark," his estate at Ossining, and died at his winter home in Phoenix.

WILLIAM KINGSLAND MACY (1889 -1961), tea merchant and Congressman. Macy, son of JIC member George H. Macy, was president of his father's Union Pacific Tea Co. 1919-22 and a partner at Abbott, Hoppin & Company, brokers. He served as state and Suffolk County Republican chair, and, from 1947-51, U. S. congressman from New York. He served on New York's Board of Regents for twelve years and was an active opponent of New York Gov. Dewey. In 1912 he married Julia A. Dick, daughter of JIC member John Henry Dick. Macy inherited Moss Cottage at Jekyll Island from his father and lived at Islip, Long Island, where his former estate is now part of Hecksher State Park.

JOHN MAGEE (born 1867; JIC member 1893-1908), coal executive. Magee was president and director of Fall Brook Coal Company. He married in 1891 Florence Seeley. They lived at Lake Wampus near Mt. Kisco, New York, and his office was in Corning, New York. Their home was robbed of more than $7,500 of valuables in 1915 as the servants slept.

ARTHUR HAYNESWORTH MASTEN (1855-1935), attorney. A son of Almeda Arthur Masten and James Masten, he was the nephew of President Chester Arthur, for whom he was named (the Arthurs' other sister, Malvina, married Henry Haynesworth, thus Arthur's middle name). He was an author and attorney and served as Assistant District Attorney in New York City. He was standing vigil during his uncle's last illness and had just stepped out of the room when the former president died. He lived in New York City and at "Tahauus" in the Adirondacks.

ARCHIBALD "ARCH" STEWART MAURICE (1870-1928). He was a son of JIC member Charles Stewart Maurice and Charlotte Maurice. His mother was founder of the Tioga Point Daughters of the American Revolution. He died as a result of an auto accident and is buried in Tioga Point Cemetery in Athens, Pennsylvania.

CHARLES STEWART MAURICE (1840-1924), civil engineer and bridge builder. Maurice served in the U.S. Navy during the Civil War and afterwards turned down a faculty appointment at the U. S. Naval Academy to enter his career as an engineer. In 1871 he co-founded the bridge-building firm of Kellogg and Maurice. Among those they designed and constructed were across the Tombigbee River in Alabama and a section of the Third Avenue Elevated Railway in New York. In 1884 the firm merged to form the Union Bridge Company with JIC members George S. Field, Edmund Hayes, and Thomas C. Clarke. Their projects included the Cantilever Bridge over the Niagara and the Memphis Bridge over the Mississippi. His wife, Charlotte Marshall Holbrooke (1840-1909), was a granddaughter of Josiah Marshall, a Boston merchant and trader with Hawaii and China. Among their children were JIC members Archibald and Margaret. The family lived at "Aloha" in Athens, Pennsylvania, and on Jekyll Island. His daughter, Emily, married Charles Whitney Dall in Jekyll's Faith Chapel in 1911, the only wedding of a JIC family member known to have taken place there. He built Hollybourne Cottage at Jekyll in 1890, the only home on the island built of native tabby stucco and employing Maurice's bridge-building skills to include attic trusses that allowed the downstairs rooms to be built

Albert Maurice and a friend display deer killed at Jekyll.

Top: Fowler McCormick, Sr. who divorced his first wife, Edith Rockefeller, and married the opera singer Ganna Walska. Orson Welles was said to have partially based Citizen Kane on the McCormick-Rockefeller-Walska triangle.

Bottom: Jekyll member Cyrus Hall McCormick, Jr., was called "Young Reaper" in deference to his father who invented the wheat harvester.

without beams or pillars. The Maurice family was the only one associated with the Club from its establishment in 1886 until its dissolution in 1948.

MARGARET "PEG" STEWART MAURICE (1888-1947). A daughter of JIC member Charles Stewart Maurice, she was seven years old when her family built Hollybourne Cottage. At her father's death, she formally inherited his club share but her siblings continued to enjoy Jekyll as they always had. She and her sister Marian were the only Maurice children who remained unmarried. They both requested to return to Jekyll after the end of World War II but were denied and, after the dissolution of the Club, until the end of their lives they would travel to Florida by driving through Alabama as a result of their displeasure that their beloved home had been taken from them.

EZRA BUTLER MCCAGG (1825 - 1908), attorney. McCagg, a Chicago resident, was a member of the U. S. Sanitary Commission and president of the Northwestern Sanitary Commission during the Civil War. He served as president of the commission that established Chicago's Lincoln Park. He had an extensive art and book collection but, in the Chicago fire of 1871, his home was destroyed, including the famous library and collection including the early writings and letters of the Jesuits. His first wife, Carline Ogden, died leaving a son, and he then married Therese Davis. McCagg was one of the original founding trustees of the Chicago Symphony along with JIC member N. K. Fairbank.

EDMUND WILKES MCCLAVE (1836-1911). McClave was an original member of the Club, replacing the name of John D.

Rockefeller whose brother, William, was a member. He and his wife lived in New York City with their sons, Rowland, Wilkes, Park, Donald, and Kennette. His namesake, attorney Wilkes McClave III, served as general counsel of oil refiner and marketer Tosco Corporation.

CYRUS HALL MCCORMICK, JR. (1859-1936), manufacturer. The eldest son of inventor and manufacturer Cyrus H. McCormick and Nancy Fowler McCormick, he was nicknamed "Young Reaper" in deference to his father and their profession. His father in 1831 demonstrated the world's first successful mechanical reaper and filed a patent for it in 1834. He then moved to Chicago in 1847 to serve the mid-west grain fields. By 1858, his company was the largest farm equipment manufacturer in the United States, with assets totaling over $1 million. In 1902 he merged with five other farm implement manufacturers to form the International Harvester Company. The voting power for the new company rested with the sons of two harvesting machine pioneers, Cyrus Hall McCormick, Jr. and JIC member Charles Deering, plus George Perkins, a partner of JIC member J.P. Morgan, who arranged and financed the consolidation. Cyrus, Jr. and his brother, Harold Fowler McCormick, presided over the company for its first forty years. Cyrus Jr. was president of the McCormick Harvesting Machine Company from 1884 to 1902, and president of the International Harvester Company after 1902. The Cyrus McCormick, Jr. family lived at "Walden," their estate in Lake Forest, IL. Their son, Stanley, married Katherine Dexter, daughter of JIC member Wirt Dexter and an early advocate for birth control.

Cyrus Jr.'s brother, Harold Fowler McCormick, married Edith Rockefeller, daughter of John D. and niece of JIC member William Rockefeller. They commissioned Frank Lloyd Wright to build a mansion for them in Chicago's north shore suburb of Lake Forest. They rejected his plans, however, and hired Charles Adams Platt to design their forty-four-room "Villa Turicum," an Italian villa, on two hundred and fifty acres. Built at a cost of $5 million, it was never lived in and was sold for $46,000 in 1947 and demolished in 1956. They had a son, Fowler McCormick (1898-1973), who, at the age of twenty-nine, married the fifty-year-old Anne Urquhart Potter, the former wife of James Alexander Stillman, son of JIC member James Stillman (James A. Stillman's sister was married to Percy Rockefeller, son of JIC member William) and president of National City Bank. The Stillmans were the parents-in-law of JIC member Henry P. Davison. Fowler McCormick's wife, Anne Potter Stillman, was a sister-in-law of JIC descendant Grace Goodyear Depew Potter, and the only child of coffee broker James Brown Potter (a partner in Brown Brothers and nephew of Bishop Potter) and Mary Cora Urquhart who earned society's disapproval for abandoning her family for the stage after she was befriended in London by the then-Prince of Wales (later King Edward VII). At the time Oscar Wilde wrote of her, "... the American invasion has done English society a great deal of good. American women are bright, clever, and wonderfully cosmopolitan." Evidently her daughter, Anne Potter McCormick, inherited her mother's pluck, as her fourth child was supposedly fathered by a handsome young native guide in Canada rather than by her husband. Stillman's resulting lawsuit

Henry K. McHarg, who shared his wealth with employees when he sold his railroad.

denying paternity wound its way through the courts for five years and cost almost $1 million in legal fees before the two settled out of court. Eventually, however, the Stillmans divorced and Anne married Fowler McCormick, who was widely assumed to be the child's real father even though he had only been a teenager when the boy was conceived. His parents divorced in 1921 during the Stillmans' public feud and the elder Fowler McCormick then married the Polish actress and opera singer Ganna Walska. Orson Welle's *Citizen Kane* was said to be partially based on the McCormick-Rockefeller-Walska triangle.

WILLEY SOLON MCCREA (1858-1927), utility executive. McCrea was treasurer of the People's Gas Light and Coal Company of Chicago and an early proponent of light harness racing. He was an avid bird watcher and an associate of the American Ornithologists' Union from 1922—1927. He contributed funding to provide food for Canada geese, and was survived by his third wife, Vera, a daughter and several grandchildren.

HENRY KING MCHARG (1851 -1941), banker and railroad president. McHarg was president of the Atlanta, Knoxville & Northern Railroad which he reorganized and sold to the Louisville & Nashville Railroad when he gave a year's salary to all its officers and a month's salary to all its employees. He was president of the Detroit and Mackinac Railroad Company until his death, as well as a director of the New York, Ontario & Western Railroad. In 1906, when he sold the Virginia and Southwestern to the Southern Railroad, he commandeered a "Santa Special" delivering gifts to all employees, including a full year's salary to senior officials, one month's salary to all lower employees who had been with the company for at least a year, and gifts totaling more than $50,000 to the others. His son, Henry K., Jr., was a vice president of the Detroit and Mackinac Railroad. He lived in Stamford, Connecticut, and died at the Mountain Lake Club near Lake Wales, Florida, where he had been on holiday for six weeks. His will gave $3 million to charities.

GORDON MCKAY (1821 -1903), inventor and shoe manufacturer. McKay was a first cousin of JIC member Wirt Dexter. He began in a manufacturing machine-shop then purchased a sewing machine invention. He proceeded to improve the invention with adaptations that allowed stitching of heels and toes and began to manufacture shoes using the device. During the Civil War his plants worked around the clock to produce shoes (each machine could turn out six hundred pairs a day). His royalties alone amounted to more than $750,000 annually and, by the time he retired in 1895, his fortune was estimated at $40 million. McKay had been divorced from his first wife for almost forty years when, in 1878, he married Minnie, his housekeeper's daughter, while in his late fifties (she was twenty-one). Having had two sons, they divorced in 1890 but he excluded the young boys from his will, believing that they were not his children. The former couple remained friendly, however, and McKay brought her, her mother, and her sons to see him when he joined the Club the following year. In 1892, he built "Indian Mound," his cottage at Jekyll, which was to become the Rockefeller home. In 1899, his ex-wife, Minnie, married Baron Adolph von Bruning,

Gordon McKay's cottage at Jekyll as it originally appeared when built in 1892. His much-younger wife seemed to be more attracted to his $40 million than to him and McKay doubted that he was the father of their children. He sold his cottage to William Rockefeller, who enlarged the home and renamed it "Indian Mound Cottage."

secretary to the German embassy in Washington, where McKay had given her a home. The newly married couple was given a wedding present of $100,000 by McKay. He stayed close to his former housekeeper/mother-in-law and her remaining daughter and they often visited him in Newport (and once came to Jekyll as his guests). McKay died at Newport having established the McKay Institute in Rhode Island "for the education of negro boys." He left Harvard $1 million outright, along with eighty percent of the annual net income of his estate. Harvard attempted to divert the funds to M.I.T. but subsequent lawsuits forced Harvard to use McKay's bequest to establish the Harvard Engineering School. There is still a McKay Laboratory at Harvard.

ALLAN MCLANE (1864 - 1940), attorney. His grandfather served as U. S. senator and secretary of state, secretary of the treasury, and minister to England under President Jackson. The JIC member was an attorney who served a partial term as associate justice in Baltimore and Harford Counties. He married in 1890 Augusta, daughter of Henry James. Among their children was Eleanor, who married as her second husband JIC member J. Hopkins Smith. McLane died at his home, "Sycamore Lodge," in Green Spring Valley, Maryland, where he had retired in 1920.

CHARLES SENFF MCVEIGH (1883 -1962), attorney. He was senior partner at the New York law firm of Morris & McVeigh, specializing in trusts and estates. McVeigh served as a trustee of the United States Trust Company, the Achelis Foundation, the Lincoln Ellsworth Foundation, and the Bodman Foundation. He founded the American Wildlife Institute in 1935 and was a founder and trustee of

Top: The Washington, DC, home of Cissy Medill Patterson, publisher of the Washington Times-Herald. It was the temporary home of President and Mrs. Coolidge during renovations to the White House in 1927 and the President received Charles Lindbergh there after his historic flight.

Right: Joseph Medill surrounded by his grandchildren: Eleanor "Cissy" Patterson, publisher of the Washington Times-Herald; Joseph Medill McCormick, U. S. Senator; Robert R. McCormick, Publisher of the Chicago Tribune and founder of WGN Radio; and Joseph M. Patterson, founder of the New York Daily News.

the Ducks Unlimited Foundation. He married in 1915 Alice Bacon and among their four sons was Charles, Jr., who joined his father's law firm. In 1951 the senior McVeigh was the trustee for the sale of his aunt's home, "Knollwood," in Syosset, Long Island, which he had developed, to former King Zog of Albania and his half-American wife. News accounts reported that McVeigh was paid with "a bucket of diamonds and rubies."

JOSEPH MEDILL (1823 -1899), newspaper publisher. Medill was mayor of Chicago immediately after the great fire. He established the *Cleveland Leader* and owned the *Chicago Tribune.* Medill was the first person to name his national party "Republican" and was an early proponent of Abraham Lincoln for President and for emancipation of slaves. In 1889 he pushed for the annexation of communities surrounding Chicago, bringing its total population above one million and thus secured the World's Fair. He married in 1852 Katharine Patrick of Philadelphia and one of their grandsons, Joseph Medill Patterson Albright, was the husband of the United States' first female secretary of state, Madeleine Albright. Medill's daughter, Katherine, married Ambassador Robert S. McCormick, first cousin of JIC member Cyrus McCormick, Jr. Katherine and Robert McCormick's son, Joseph Medill McCormick, was a United States senator who married U. S. Congresswoman Ruth Hanna, a daughter of his fellow senator Mark Hanna. JIC member Joseph Medill's other daughter, Eleanor, married Robert Patterson, Jr. and they inherited the *Chicago Tribune.* The Pattersons were the parents of the famed Eleanor Medill "Cissy" Patterson, owner of the *Washington Times-Herald,* while their son was Joseph Medill Patterson, the Pulitzer prize-winning founder of the *New York Daily News,* whose daughter, Alicia (wife of Ambassador Harry Guggenheim) founded *Newsday.*

ALBERT GOODSELL MILBANK (1873 -1949), attorney and corporate official. He was a partner at the law firm of Milbank & Tweed and also served as chairman of the Borden Company. He co-chaired with JIC member William Rockefeller the United War Work Campaign and was a trustee of the Pierpont Morgan Library. He and his family lived at Lloyd Harbor in Huntington, Long Island, where he served as the town's first mayor. Milbank was a trustee of Princeton University, his alma mater, and president of a charity established by his cousin, the Milbank Fund, in honor of their great-grandparents. He was decorated by Serbia for war work and Britain awarded him an honorary Order of the British Empire in 1946. He married Marjorie E. Robbins, who died in 1933. Milbank's funeral at St. Bartholomew's was attended by more than 1,000 people. His mother, Georgiana Goodsell Milbank, was a family relation of both Mrs. Oliver B. Jennings and Mrs. William Rockefeller.

GERRISH HILL MILLIKEN (1877 - 1947), manufacturer. Upon graduation from college, he joined Deering, Milliken & Company, textile selling agents, where his father was controlling partner. He succeeded as head of the firm in 1920 at his father's death and remained in that position until his own death. Milliken was also chairman and president of many southern textile mills. His family were summer residents of Mt. Desert Island, Maine. Milliken died while playing golf at Southampton, Long Island, with his son, Roger, who succeeded him as president of the company. He married in 1913 Agnes Malcolm, daughter of James Gayley, who was vice president of U. S. Steel. Among their children was a daughter, Anne, who married Baron Mario Franchetti. The Franchetti's grandson, Cody, was featured in the television special, "Born Rich," in which he stated, "I find guilt [over wealth] absolutely senseless. It's basically for old women and nuns."

JOHN GODFREY MOORE (1847- 1899), financier. Moore was president of the Mutual Union Telegraph Company. After fierce competition, in 1882 Western Union was forced to lease existing Mutual Union lines for a period of ninety-nine years. Moore was elected a director of Western Union and took a one year's European sabbatical before founding the New York City banking house of Moore & Schley with JIC member Grant Barney Schley. In 1886 he purchased a seat on the New York Stock Exchange and acquired controlling interest in the Chase National Bank. His firm represented the Havemeyers, the Rockefellers, J. Pierpont Morgan, and William C. Whitney. He successfully challenged in court the nation's first income tax which was declared unconstitutional. Moore was also a yachtsman and his country estate was "Far From the Wolf" at Winter Harbor, Maine. Moore hosted Thomas B. Reed, Speaker of the U. S. House of Representatives, when he visited Jekyll in 1899 at the same time President McKinley visited the Island. Among Moore's children was Ruth who married Arthur Hamilton Lee, Viscount Lee of Fareham. The Viscount was a good friend of U. S. President Theodore Roosevelt and was an honorary member of the Rough Riders. He was British military attaché in Washington, served in Parliament, and rose through the ranks of government service. He and his wife purchased, restored, and furnished the Chequers Estate which they gave to the British nation in 1921. Their extensive art collection was bequeathed to the Courtauld Institute of Art.

VICTOR MORAWETZ (1859- 1938), attorney. His Austrian-born father was a physician. The son practiced law in New York City with Seward, Guthrie, Morawetz & Steele. He was counsel for several railways, represented J.P. Morgan & Company in several railroad reorganizations, and was one of the lawyers who incorporated U. S. Steel. Morawetz represented Andrew Carnegie in complicated railroad litigation and was chairman of the board of the Atchison, Topeka & Santa Fe Railroad 1896-1909. He authored many law books and, at his retirement, moved to a large plantation near Charleston, South Carolina, where he restored a 1730 home. He died in Charleston with no children and his substantial estate was left in trust to his widow, then was divided between the Boys Club of New York, the Medical Society of South Carolina, Roper Hospital in Charleston, and Johns Hopkins Hospital.

JOHN HILL MORGAN (1870 -1945), attorney. Morgan was a partner in the law firm of Rumsey & Morgan. He was a member of the New York Assembly 1900-03 and served as a director of several corporations. He was honorary curator of American Painting at the Yale School of Fine Arts and an author on American painting (particularly portraiture). He and his wife, Lelia, lived at "Mill Streams" in Farmington, Connecticut.

JOHN PIERPONT MORGAN (1837-1913), banker and capitalist. "Pierpont," as he was called by his family, was a

Top left: The Morgan home, now part of the J. P. Morgan Library.

Top right: J. P. Morgan's funeral cortege makes it way through New York City.

Bottom: J. P. Morgan enters the 1911 funeral of his fellow Jekyll member Cornelius Bliss.

grandson of one of the founders of Aetna Insurance Company. The grandfather purchased for his son, Pierpont's father Junius, a dry-goods business in 1836, the same year of his marriage to Juliet Pierpont. At the grandfather's death in 1847, his estate of more than $1 million allowed his family to move to London, then enroll young Pierpont in a Swiss boarding institute where he displayed an unusual talent for mathematics. He returned to the U.S. and worked in his father's business until, in 1859, he supposedly gambled the firm's entire capital on a boatload of coffee. Although he made a substantial profit, he had not secured permission for such a risky endeavor and ventured out on his own when the firm's more conservative partners denied him a partnership. In 1861 Pierpont married Amelia Sturges who was so ill with tuberculosis that he physically had to carry her downstairs for the ceremony. He did the same throughout their honeymoon in the Mediterranean but, four months later, she was dead. His will, executed more than fifty years later, included a substantial endowment for a rest home in her name. Four years later his father capitalized a new firm for Pierpont and approved of his marriage to Frances "Fanny" Tracy, daughter of a respectable attorney. The marriage was successful in producing children – J. P., Jr. (known as "Jack"), Louisa, Juliet (who married a great-grandson of Alexander Hamilton), and Anne – but there was little warmth between its partners. She kept their homes running smoothly and turned a blind eye to his extramarital affairs. In 1902 Morgan hired Charles McKim, partner of Stanford White, to design his library at 36th Street and Madison Avenue. Morgan then began in earnest his pursuit of the very best in books and art. Morgan owned three of fewer than fifty Gutenberg Bibles in existence. He became president of the Metropolitan Museum of Art in 1904 and remained in the post until his death. In 1907 he personally intervened to avert a financial crisis which threatened to destroy the U. S. economy, using every weapon at his disposal to force the nation's bankers to join him in the effort. Although daughter Louisa was his favorite child, the youngest, Anne, was most like him. She founded the Colony Club (for women only) and traveled extensively with Elsie de Wolfe and her lover, Bessie Marbury. Though Anne was decorated for her fundraising efforts on behalf of the French between the World Wars, her father ensured that the openly-homosexual Marbury, whom he viewed as a negative influence on his daughter, did not receive a similar honor. Pierpont was an active JIC member and, among other efforts, was among the first members to live at "Sans Souci," the nation's first condominium, housing apartments for members who did not wish to build their own homes on the Island. His successive yachts, all named the *Corsair*, were frequent visitors to Jekyll. Six of the ten pallbearers at Morgan's funeral were JIC members. After his death, when it became public knowledge that his estate was valued at $77.5 million (not counting his art collection), John D. Rockefeller exclaimed admiringly, "And to think he wasn't even a rich man!"

JOHN PIERPONT MORGAN, JR. (1867 -1943), capitalist and banker. "Jack" was chairman of the board of J. P. Morgan & Company, and chairman of the board of U. S. Steel from its founding until 1932 when he became a director. He followed his father in many respects, including his JIC membership, where Jack served as president of the Club from 1933-38 and attempted to introduce a more business-like approach to its operations. He married in 1890 Jane Norton Grew who died in1925; they had two sons and two daughters. Morgan was a director of many corporations and was decorated by the governments of Italy, Belgium, France, Japan, England, as well as by the Pope. They lived at Matinicock Point in Glen Cove, Long Island, in London, and at Wall Hall in Watford, England. In July of 1915, he and his wife were entertaining at their Glen Cove home Sir Cecil Spring-Rice, the British Ambassador to the U. S., when a gunman made his way into the house. He was forcing the Morgan daughters upstairs at gunpoint when the diminutive Mrs. Morgan threw herself on top of him. Jack Morgan received two bullet wounds while subduing the gunman, who also carried dynamite in his pocket. Two weeks later he committed suicide in prison. Although Pierpont Morgan's will left almost $10 million to charitable organizations, his collections were left intact to his son, Jack, who lent them to the Metropolitan Museum of Art from 1914-1916 before giving most of them outright to the Museum. He retained only the books, drawings, and manuscripts which were opened to view by the public beginning in 1924 at his father's former library. Although an Episcopalian, his friend Pope Pius XI created him a Papal Knight. Jack Morgan died at the Gasparilla Hotel in Boca Grande, Florida, where he had gone to escape the northern winter. His son, Harry, married a great-granddaughter of President John Q. Adams and was one of the two original named partners at the investment banking house of Morgan, Stanley & Company.

WILLIAM FELLOWES MORGAN (1860 - 1943), warehouseman. Morgan began as a stock broker then founded a cold storage business. He was chairman of the board of Merchant's Refrigerating Company and a director of several corporations, including Savannah Sugar Refining Company. Morgan was a member of the New Jersey legislature 1905-07 from Short Hills and later lived in New York City. He was a trustee of Columbia and of American University in Beirut as well as a trustee of the Cathedral of St. John the Divine. He and his wife, Emma Leavitt, had a son and two daughters. One daughter married Frederick Pruyn (son of JIC member Robert Pruyn) then David M. Goodrich; the other married Cleveland E. Dodge. Dodge, a grandson of both Anson Phelps and William E. Dodge who co-founded the Phelps Dodge Foundation, had a particular interest in the mid-east where he sent two of his four children to school: Bayard to the American University at Beirut and Elizabeth to Robert College at Constantinople (where her father was chairman of the board). After World War I, Bayard Dodge became president of the American University at Beirut. His wife's grandfather, Daniel Bliss, was the University's first president. Bayard Dodge's son, David, was acting president of the University in 1982 when he was kidnapped and held hostage for a year. He is now chairman of the board of the Near East Foundation. His sister, Grace Dodge Guthrie, wrote *Legacy to Lebanon*, a history of the American Community School in Beirut. Morgan's grandson, Dr. Fellowes Morgan Pruyn, gave substantial acreage near Chappaqua, New York,

J. P. "Jack" Morgan, Jr., who served as president of the Jekyll Island Club from 1933-1938. His wife, Jane Norton Morgan, was an accomplished amateur artist who sketched her surroundings at Jekyll Island.

Above: Jekyll's gamekeeper and his dogs.

Right: Helen Hartley Jenkins rides with Dr. Donald McEachern in a "red bug," an early and popular form of mechanized transportation at Jekyll, in 1929.

as a bird sanctuary and arboretum.

RAY MORRIS (1878- 1961), banker. A son of Luzon B. Morris, Governor of Connecticut from 1893 to 1895, Morris was a partner in Brown Brothers Harriman and president of the Investment Bankers Association of America in 1926 as well as a director of many corporations. He married in 1906 Katharine Grinnell; their son, Grinnell Morris, married a daughter of JIC member Frederic R. Kellogg. The Morris' daughter, Virginia, married Nicholas Biddle.

STANLEY GRAFTON MORTIMER (1890 -1947), broker and sportsman. For a few years Mortimer was associated with the brokerage firm of Russell, Miller & Company but then turned to sports. He virtually dominated racquetball between 1915 and 1931, winning the national championships in 1916, 1923, 1926, and 1930, and with Clarence Pell won the national doubles championship in 1915, from 1921 to 1925, and in 1927, 1928, and 1931. He and his wife, Katharine, were active members of Tuxedo Park. One of their daughters, Katharine, first married Oliver Biddle then tennis champion Francis X. Shields who, with his former wife, Princess Marina Torlonia di Civitella-Cesi, were the grandparents of actress Brooke Shields. Mortimer's son, Stanley G., Jr., married Babe Cushing, later the wife of CBS president Bill Paley. Mortimer shared an aunt, Elizabeth Livingston Mortimer, with first lady Eleanor Roosevelt.

MURRY NELSON (born 1830; JIC member 1888-1899), corn merchant. Nelson was an early settler of Chicago where he was a corn merchant and a director of the Chicago Board of Trade 1863-64. With two partners he formed the firm of Vincent, Nelson &

Company. They built the National Elevator Company in 1867 and continued in business until the great fire of 1871 when their elevator was burned. They re-built in 1871-72 with a storage capacity of one million bushels – four times their former capacity – said to be the only fire-proof grain elevator in Chicago. After the fire, the Relief Aid Society appointed several committee chairs, including Murry Nelson and his fellow JIC members Wirt Dexter and N. K. Fairbank, to distribute assistance and re-build Chicago. After his partners' retirement and death, Murry Nelson continued the business as the largest stockholder. Nelson married Catherine Thatcher and their daughter, Josephine, married a son of JIC member N. K. Fairbank. Nelson lived with them as an older man and reminisced for *The New York Times* in 1916 (when he was eighty-six) about the Mexican War of 1846 and his friendship with Abraham Lincoln. Nelson was a trustee of Antioch College in Ohio.

HORATIO VICTOR NEWCOMB (1844 - 1911), capitalist. Born in Louisville, Kentucky, Newcomb began as a cotton merchant and succeeded his father as president of the Louisville & Nashville Railroad Company. In 1880 he organized and was president of the U. S. National Bank, whose directors included General U. S. Grant and JIC member Henry B. Hyde. He was also a partner at the banking firm of Warren, Newcomb & Company in New York City. He lived on Fifth Avenue and had an estate in Stroudsburg, Pennsylvania. After acquiring a fortune, he suffered a nervous breakdown, then became addicted to the narcotic chloral. Under its influence he threatened to kill Henry Flagler and announced that the explorer Henry M. Stanley planned to kill Newcomb. He was committed to a sanitarium where he lived for ten years with no legal rights. After Newcomb had regained his sanity and his freedom, he fought a long battle in the courts for his extensive properties which had been held in trust. He also brought suit for separation against his wife which included scandalous allegations against her. His business acumen returned in full and he greatly added to his wealth before his death in Atlantic City, New Jersey, at his summer home.

HOFFMAN NICKERSON (1888 -1965), author and biographer. Nickerson was elected a member of the New York Assembly in 1916, the same year he married Ruth Comstock. A recognized author of military history and biography, his works included *American Rich,* commissioned by his associate, Nelson Rockefeller. In another book, Nickerson described Horatio Gates, American commander of the Northern Department, as "a snob of the first water" who possessed "an unctuously pious way." He had two sons by his first wife, then married Jane Soames in 1938. They had two sons and lived at Yellow Cote House in Oyster Bay, Long Island. His son, Eugene, who ran unsuccessfully for governor of New York, was the judge who presided over the Abner Louima police brutality proceedings that led to the conviction of six New York City police officers.

RICHARD LIVINGSTON OGDEN (born 1822; JIC member 1886 - 1892). Ogden married in 1854 Isabelle Pratt in New York City then fought in the Civil War before settling in San Francisco. There he was manager of the Kimball Manufacturing Company until the 1870 depression bankrupted the firm. Ogden was commodore of the San Francisco Yacht Club in 1875 but his fortune was greatly

Palmer Square in Princeton, NJ. Edgar Palmer's gift of $4.5 million began the rehabilitation of downtown Princeton.

impacted by his firm's financial decline. He was one of the original incorporators of the Jekyll Island Club and, in need of income, served as its paid superintendent for its first season. His youngest child, Isabelita, married in 1883 Richard Henry Pease, who was president of the Goodyear Rubber Company of San Francisco. Pease's son, Richard, Jr., succeeded his father as president of the Goodyear Rubber Company's San Francisco operations.

HELEN SLADE OGILVIE (Mrs. Clinton Ogilvie) (JIC

member 1917-25), philanthropist. She was a daughter of Jarvis Slade of Boston. Her husband, Clinton Ogilvie (1838-1900), whom she married in 1872, was an artist widely known for his landscapes. His widow built the deanery of the Cathedral of St. John the Divine in his memory and was known for her collection of Oriental rugs. Their daughter, Ida, was a well-known geologist who was among the first women to receive her Ph.D. from Columbia University in 1903 before becoming a professor at Barnard College. She was Barnard's first chairman of the geology department and died in 1963.

JAMES FRANCIS O'SHAUGHNESSEY (JIC member 1887-94; rejoined 1899-1914), developer. In 1888 O'Shaughnessey purchased Sea Island, Georgia, from the heirs of James Hamilton Couper to use as a hunting preserve. It was used mainly for grazing livestock until 1921, when a local group of businessmen led by Howard Coffin purchased it and divided the property for development. Coffin's cousin, JIC member Alfred William Jones, was his partner in developing Sea Island.

EDGAR PALMER (1880- 1943), manufacturer. The son of JIC member Stephen S. Palmer, he was chairman of the board of the New Jersey Zinc Company. In 1910 he married Zilph Hayes. He had been president of the company from 1912 to 1927 before becoming chairman. He lived in Princeton, New Jersey, with offices in New York City. In 1913 he gave the Palmer Memorial Stadium to Princeton in memory of his father (dedicated the day of the Princeton-Yale football game) and also gave a dormitory to the Stevens Institute of Technology. Palmer was commodore of the American Yacht Club and he gave his first yacht, *Guinevere*, a three-masted schooner, to the U. S. Navy. It was sunk off Brest, France, in 1918 and he built a duplicate of the same name to participate in a trans-Atlantic race sponsored by the King of Spain. At the outbreak of World War II he gave that yacht as well to the U. S. Navy. His one child, Zilph, married Walter B. Devereux, III, whose father was an early developer of Aspen and built the Hotel Colorado. Palmer contributed $4.5 million to rehabilitate the central business district of Princeton, New Jersey. His daughter gave the Rye marshlands to Westchester County in 1967, but her family gave their house, outbuildings, and surrounding twenty-three acres to the Methodist Church for a regional headquarters and conference center. Palmer's will left $6 million to family members and to Princeton.

STEPHEN SQUIRES PALMER (1853-1913), manufacturer. Palmer was president of the New Jersey Zinc Company from 1892 till 1912 when he became chairman of the board. He built the largest smelting plant in America at Lehigh Gap, Pennsylvania, and established the town of Palmerton (to take advantage of the anthracite deposits to be mined there), although he was said not to be pleased that the town was named for him. He held many corporate directorships and built the church at Palmerton as a memorial to his wife for the use of his three thousand employees and their families. Palmer also gave the choir and the parish house of All Angels' Church in New York City and contributed $500,000 to his alma mater, Princeton, to build a laboratory. He married Susan Sanders Price in 1879 and they were the parents of JIC member Edgar Palmer. A scholarship in Palmer's name was established in 1924 at the Stevens Institute of Technology. There is also a high school in Palmerton, Pennsylvania, named for him built by funds from the company in his memory. He died at his second home in Redland, California.

KATHERINE "KATE" RENNETT ALLERTON PAPIN (Mrs. Francis Sidney Papin and Mrs. Hugo Richards Johnstone) (1863-1937). Born in Chicago, she was the daughter of JIC member Samuel Waters Allerton. She became the Club's first female member when she acquired the share of her father. She married Dr. Francis S. Papin, then JIC member Hugo Richards Johnstone. She lived on Prairie Avenue in Chicago and at "Folly," the Allertons' summer home. Johnstone married secondly Alice Child, widow of John Purroy Mitchel, mayor of New York City from 1914 to 1917, who was known as "the Boy Wonder of New York."

CHARLES HENRY PARKHURST (Honorary) (1842 – 1933), Presbyterian clergyman and civic reformer. He was the only honorary member ever elected and his financial supporters included JIC member James A. Scrymser. From 1880 until 1918 Parkhurst was rector of Madison Square Presbyterian Church in New York City. In 1891 he became president of the Society for Prevention of Crime and was a highly-visible proponent of ridding New York City of crime and vice. He was subpoenaed before a grand jury after accusing municipal officials of corruption and was known for personally visiting crime locations in the streets. One of the many books he authored was *Our Fight With Tammany*. Joseph Choate, U. S. Ambassador to the Court of St. James, called Parkhurst "the moral

The Jekyll Island Club dining room afforded discreet opportunities for both social and business transactions.

ruler of the town." Parkhurst died after a fall from a second floor window while sleepwalking at the age of ninety-one. Near the end of his life, Parkhurst insisted, "You cannot legislate the human race into heaven."

GEORGE ELTON PARKS (JIC member 1930 - 34), jewelry manufacturer. He was a son of jewelry silversmith manufacturer George Winant Parks (1856 – 1929) and Helen Roberts Parks of Providence, Rhode Island. He married Helen Judson in 1915. His sister's husband, Elbert Spicer Barlow, supervised the construction of the Metropolitan Life Insurance Tower at One Madison Avenue in New York City.

DUNCAN DUNBAR PARMLY (born 1849; JIC member 1897-98), banker and railroad official. His father was the long-time minister of the First Baptist Church of Jersey City, New Jersey. The son was a director of the St. Louis, Iron Mountain and Southern Railroad before it became a part of the Missouri Pacific System. Parmly was then a founder and senior partner of the New York City banking firm of Marquand & Parmly. In 1893 he ended his partnership and became president of the Phenix National Bank of New York City. Phenix was bought in 1905 by JIC member J. P. Morgan and by August Belmont. Parmly lived at Middletown, New Jersey.

JAMES CRESSON PARRISH (1840 – 1926), philanthropist. A son of Isaac Parrish and Sarah Longstreth Parrish, he was a financial backer of Thomas A. Edison. His brother, Samuel Longstreth Parrish, founded the Parrish Art Museum in Southampton, where the Parrish family lived, and donated to it

his extensive art collection. In 1902 James C. Parrish financed a fireproof brick wing on the north side of the building that became the museum's new exhibition hall. He was the second husband of Emma S. Thorn, a granddaughter of Commodore Vanderbilt and formerly the wife of Edward King (by whom she had two children, including Louise Thorn King who married JIC member Alexander Baring). They had two children, James C. Parrish and Helen Parrish, and lived at "Zee en Duin" in Southampton, Long Island.

ROBERT WARDEN PATERSON (1855 - 1917), shipping merchant. He was born in Scotland, a son of John Paterson and Margaret Warden. In the U. S. he became a shipping merchant with Paterson, Downing & Company, purveyor of naval stores, then Paterson, Boardman & Company, dry goods merchants. A director of the Manhattan Bank, his wife was Marie Louise Fahys.

ANTHONY JOSEPH DREXEL PAUL (1884 -1958), estate executor and sportsman. Paul grew up at "Woodcrest" in Radnor, Pennsylvania, which was later sold to the Dorrance family of Campbell's Soup. He graduated from Harvard and entered the banking firm of Cassatt & Company for several years before leaving to manage his grandfather's estate. Paul was a nationally-ranked polo player and in 1908 married Isabel Biddle. Among their children was Anne whose husband, Maitland Alexander, was moderator of the Presbyterian Church and a founder of Westminster Theological Seminary. Paul was a Philadelphia philanthropist and community activist and chairman of the board of the Drexel Institute. He lived at "Woodcrest," designed by Horace Trumbauer, who designed "The Elms," the Berwind mansion at Newport. His father's sister, Mary Dahlgren Paul, married William Waldorf Astor, U. S. Ambassador to Italy, who moved to England and was created the 1st Viscount Astor. His grandfather, Anthony Joseph Drexel, was a banker, philanthropist, founder of Drexel University, partner of J. P. Morgan, and financial advisor to President U. S. Grant. Paul's son, A. J. D. Paul, Jr., established a Drexel alumni award in his father's name. His aunt, Sister Katharine Drexel (1858-1955), was canonized in 2000 as only the second American-born saint.

THOMAS WILLITS PEARSALL (1838-1909), railroad executive. Pearsall was vice-president of the International Great Northern Railroad. The town of Pearsall, Texas, was named for him in 1881 when its first passenger train, the Great Northern, served the area. His sister, Charlotte, was the wife of Edwin Thorne and mother of JIC member Oakleigh Thorne. They had at least one son, Paul S., who lived at "Black Rock" in Washington, D.C., and died in 1919 at the age of forty-nine. At the time it was said he had inherited "a large fortune from his father."

ALFRED WALDEN PELL (1833-1901), attorney. Pell graduated from Harvard law school in 1855 and practiced law in New York City.

FRANKLIN DWIGHT PELTON (born 1861; JIC member 1902-06). He was a son of attorney and U. S. Congressman Guy Ray Pelton (1824-1890), who died attempting to climb Mary's Mountain in Yellowstone National Park, and of Lucy Carter Pelton. In 1907 he married Elizabeth Gordon, the divorced wife of Dan R. Hanna, son of U. S. Senator Mark Hanna, who visited Jekyll in 1899 with President McKinley.

PHILLIPS PHOENIX (1834 - 1921), attorney and estate executor. Phoenix was a graduate of Harvard law school but practiced only a few years before retiring to manage his family's estate. His father, J. Phillips Phoenix, was a congressman from New York City who married Mary, a daughter of Stephen Whitney, whose fortune at his death was second only to that of John Jacob Astor. Phillips Phoenix's first cousins were society architect Whitney Warren and Mary Warren, who married JIC member Robert Goelet III.

JOHN FRED PIERSON (1839 -1932), soldier and manufacturer. Pierson was a brigadier general in the Union Army who was shot and captured until released in a prisoner exchange. After the War he was president of Ramapo Foundry & Wheel Works and Ramapo Manufacturing Company in New York City. He married S. Augusta Rhodes in 1869 and among their children was son John who married Virginia Land, daughter of the chief justice of the Louisiana Supreme Court.

HENRY KIRKE PORTER (1840 -1921), manufacturer. Porter was a Congressman from Pittsburgh and president of H. K. Porter Company, locomotive manufacturers. He married Mrs. Annie de Camp Hegeman in 1875; she died in 1925. Porter was an original trustee of the Carnegie Institute of Pittsburgh and a founder of the American Academy in Rome. They lived at "Oak Manor" at Oakland, Pennsylvania. His widow, along with Samuel L. Parrish (brother of a JIC member), gave the land for William Merritt Chase's summer art school at Shinnecock Hills on Long Island.

Porter died at his residence in Washington, D.C., at the corner of 16th & I St., N.W., which his step-daughter, Miss Hegeman, gave to the Smithsonian. It is now the location of the Motion Picture Association.

HAROLD IRVING PRATT (1877 -1939), investment manager. His father, Charles Pratt, was a founder of Standard Oil and the founder of the Pratt Institute in Brooklyn. The son was chairman of Charles Pratt & Company in New York City. His wife, Harriet Barnes Pratt, was president of Hortus, Inc., the company in charge of floral planting and landscaping for the New York World's Fair. She was a trusted advisor to the White House on decorations and the acquisition of furnishings from President Coolidge to President Truman. Eleanor Roosevelt named her the first chairman of an official committee formed for that purpose and she left her valuable papers to the White House Collection. Pratt's family lived on their 2,000 acre estate on Long Island Sound, boasting one of America's finest private gardens. He and his wife gave the land in Glen Cove for the city hall, post office, and other public buildings. He died at "Welwyn," his summer home in Glen Cove. His sister-in-law, Ruth Baker Pratt, was the first female member of New York City's board of aldermen and a member of the U. S. Congress from New York 1929-33.

BERNON SHELDON PRENTICE (1882 – 1948), investment banker. A Harvard graduate, Prentice was a partner at Dominick & Dominick and a director of several corporations. He was the singles champion of lawn tennis at the Seabright Tennis and Cricket Club for twenty-five consecutive years from 1902 until 1927. He was

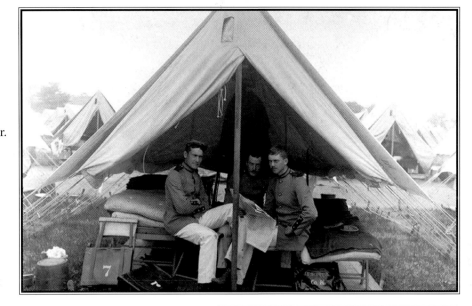

Top: J. Fred Pierson on the left in battle camp.

Right: J. P. "Jack" Morgan, Jr., with Bernon Prentice, both of whom served as president of the Jekyll Island Club. Prentice was a lawn tennis champion and served as chairman of the American Davis Cup Committee.

chairman of the American Davis Cup Committee and a non-playing member of America's Davis Cup team. During World War I he organized the Red Cross ambulance service on the Italian front and was later decorated by the Italian and French governments for his work. Prentice chaired the Amundsen-Ellsworth Polar Flight of 1925 and the Amundsen flight over the North Pole in 1926. His wife, Clara, was a daughter of JIC member James W. Ellsworth. She died of pneumonia at Savannah, Georgia, in 1929, on the way to Havana with her husband. Their son, Sheldon, was killed in action in the Pacific in 1945. In 1932 the widowed Prentice married Josephine McFadden, widow of a prominent Philadelphian. They lived at Holmdale, New York; his office was in New York City. In 1930, he was a passenger in a car driven by JIC member Frank H. Goodyear, Jr., when it wrecked. Prentice was injured and pinned in the wreckage; Goodyear died as a result of his injuries. Prentice served as the last president of the Jekyll Island Club and did everything in his power to prevent the Club's failure, including opposing condemnation by the State of Georgia. A collector of American and English paintings, he died at the "Homestead" in Virginia, and his widow lived until 1952.

HARLEY THOMAS PROCTER (1847-1920), scientist and advertiser. A son of the founder of Procter & Gamble, he was the company's head of sales and a brother of JIC member William Alexander Procter. He joined the firm in 1868 when it was a small local enterprise with three salesmen and a total advertising budget of three thousand dollars. Harley Procter named the company's soap product "Ivory" from the Biblical verse in Psalm 45: "All thy garments smell of myrrh, and aloes, and cassia, out of the ivory palaces whereby they have made thee glad." He convinced the board to spend money for advertising and in 1882 a budget of eleven thousand dollars was expended for their original "99 and 44/100 percent pure" slogan (coined from chemists' reports having obtained the number by adding the results then averaging). He designed the first wrapper for Ivory and patented the notched bar which serves as its identification. His advertising was distinguished by warm, friendly copy, with some ads featuring verse and others humor. All the ads were well-illustrated with many of the pictures appearing in color. In other campaigns, he used testimonials signed by leading chemists and commissioned the best illustrators of the day for his magazine advertisements. He retired from active business at the age of forty-five to travel and lived in Paris, London, and Egypt. His son, William, served as a P&G director.

WILLIAM ALEXANDER PROCTER (JIC member 1895-1898; died 1907), manufacturer. In 1837, William Procter and James Gamble married two sisters, beginning a partnership that would continue for well over a century. William's son, William A., served as the first president of the newly-incorporated (1890) Procter & Gamble. William A. committed suicide by shooting himself in the mouth at his home in Glendale near Cincinnati and his son became president of the company. A foundation in his name still pays the salaries of Episcopal chaplains at Princeton and Rutgers. He was the father of JIC members Harley Thomas Procter and William Cooper Procter. In 1987 P&G celebrated its 150th anniversary. The Company ranked as the second oldest company

Left: William Procter and James Gamble, who married sisters and formed Procter & Gamble. Procter's two sons and a grandson were Jekyll members.

Bottom: An early Procter & Gamble factory. Its two founders each pledged $3,596.47 to start the company that today has twelve billion dollar brands in its portfolio.

among the fifty largest Fortune 500 companies. Its brands include Pampers, Tide, Charmin, Tampax, Pantene, Bounty, Crest, Folgers, Pringles, Head & Shoulders, Ivory, Oil of Olay, Max Factor, Bold, Zest, Hugo Boss, LaCoste, Downy, Iams, Crisco, Jif, Smucker, and Lava. Procter's granddaughter, Elise Procter, married Paul Matthews, later Episcopal Bishop of New Jersey, and they founded Trinity College of Quezon City in the Philippines using Procter & Gamble stock.

WILLIAM COOPER PROCTER (1862 -1934), manufacturer and philanthropist. One month before graduating from Princeton in 1883, Procter entered the family firm, P&G, at his father's request. He became president in 1907 at his father's suicide and was chairman of the board from 1930. Under his leadership the company became the largest soap manufacturer (Ivory, Camay, Oxydol, and Lava) in the world. He added edible products beginning with Crisco, and was the first to give workers Saturday afternoon off, as well as the first to implement a profit-sharing plan for his employees and even a pension plan. He married Jane Eliza Johnston in 1889 and they had no children. He was a trustee of Princeton and a director of the New York Central Railroad. Procter gave $2.5 million to the Children's Hospital of Cincinnati. An avid golfer, he was said to have played eighteen holes in one hour.

ROBERT CLARENCE PRUYN (1847 – 1934), banker. For forty-one years Pruyn was president of the National Commercial Bank in Albany, New York. He was also president of the Albany Railway and a director of several corporations. His father was named U. S. Minister to Japan by President Lincoln and the son served as his secretary after graduating from Rutgers. Pruyn married Anna Williams in 1873 and their children included Ruth (who married a son of manufacturer B. F. Goodrich) and Frederic, who married a daughter of JIC member William Fellowes Morgan. Pruyn's summer home was Camp Santoanoni, his 12,500-acre estate in the Adirondacks. Its gate lodge was designed by William Delano, son of JIC member Eugene Delano. Pruyn advised the Episcopal Church on its finances and investments and entertained his close friend Teddy Roosevelt at his home in the Adirondacks just before he became U. S. president. His granddaughter, Ruth, first married Ogden Phipps, grandson of steel industrialist Henry Phipps and the longest-reigning member of the American Jockey Club. She then married Marshall Field III, grandson of JIC member Marshall Field. Pruyn's grandson, Dr. Fellowes Morgan Pruyn, gave substantial acreage near Chappaqua, New York, as a bird sanctuary and arboretum.

JOSEPH PULITZER (1847 – 1911), newspaper publisher. Pulitzer came to the U. S. from Hungary in 1864 and was a reporter on a German-language newspaper. In 1878 he bought the *St. Louis Dispatch* and the *St. Louis Post* and merged them into one newspaper. He was elected a member of the Missouri legislature in 1869 and a member of the U. S. Congress from New York 1885-87, but resigned after a few months. He married in 1873 Kate Davis, a second cousin of Jefferson Davis, president of the Confederacy. Pulitzer became best-known as the owner of the *New York World*, New York City's most widely-read paper at the time. He purchased it in 1883 from financier Jay Gould whose two eldest sons, George and Edwin, were JIC members. In 1887 he suffered a complete

Top: Joseph Pulitzer, owner of the New York World, the most widely-read newspaper in New York City at the time. He died on his yacht en route to Jekyll Island.

Right: Ralph Pulitzer inherited the presidency of his father's publishing empire in 1911.

breakdown from overwork and his health remained impaired for the remainder of his life. When he was in residence at his Jekyll Island cottage, built in 1897, he would pay the ferry ship's captain not to blow his whistle when approaching Jekyll's dock as it disturbed his quiet enjoyment. His wife found Jekyll too rustic and preferred more elegant locations for their social advantages. In 1903 Pulitzer endowed the Columbia University School of Journalism with an initial gift of $1 million and an agreement to contribute an additional $1 million once the school was operating. He died aboard his 1650-ton sound-proofed yacht, the *Liberty*, in the harbor of Charleston, South Carolina, on his way to Jekyll Island. Mrs. Pulitzer lived until 1927 and spent much of her time at "Villa Romaine," her home in Deauville, France. Their eldest son, Ralph, was a JIC member and also took control of the *New York World* while his brother, Joseph, became editor of the *St. Louis Post-Dispatch*. The Pulitzers also had a home in New York City as well as an estate in Bar Harbour, Maine. His will established the prestigious Pulitzer Awards.

RALPH PULITZER (1879 - 1939), newspaper publisher and author. The eldest son of JIC member Joseph Pulitzer, Ralph married Frederica Vanderbilt Webb, a granddaughter of William Henry Vanderbilt in 1905. They were divorced and in 1928 he married award-winning biographer Margaret K. Leech. Pulitzer was president of the Pulitzer Publishing Company from 1911 to 1930 and lived in Manhasset, Long Island, and in New York City.

MOSES TAYLOR PYNE (1855 - 1921), attorney and estate executor. Pyne inherited a vast estate compiled by his maternal grandfather, Moses Taylor, first president of the National City Bank of New York (succeeded by JIC member James Stillman) and the principal stockholder in the Delaware, Lackawanna and Western Railroad Company. Pyne devoted most of his adult life and much of his fortune to helping Princeton grow from a college into a university. During his thirty-six years on the Board of Trustees he did not miss a single meeting until the week before he died. He helped recruit Woodrow Wilson as president and, in 1910, refused the presidency at Wilson's retirement because he thought he could contribute more as a trustee. The University's buildings and professorships honor his total contributions of approximately $100 million and he and his wife are buried in Princeton Cemetery with their sons, Moses and Robert. The younger son, Percy Rivington Pyne II, was a banker and railroad director who died unmarried in 1929. His McKim, Mead & White-designed mansion still stands at 68th Street and Park Avenue. Moses Pyne married in 1880 Margaretta Stockton, great-great-granddaughter of Richard Stockton, a member of Princeton's first graduating class in 1748. He greatly expanded and improved their home, "Drumthwacket," and it is now the New Jersey Governor's mansion. Moses Pyne's first cousin, Constance Rivington Russell, married John G. Winant, who served as governor of New Hampshire and U. S. ambassador to the Court of St. James.

BLANCHARD RANDALL (1856 -1942), merchant and grain broker. His father was Alexander Randall, attorney general of Maryland. In 1907 the son became a senior member of Gill & Fisher, Baltimore grain merchants and brokers. He was also

St. Patrick's Cathedral, designed by Jekyll member James Renwick, Jr., was considered his finest work.

a corporate director, a trustee of Johns Hopkins University and Hospital, and chairman of the Baltimore Museum of Art. In 1902-03 Randall was president of the National Board of Trade. His wife, Susan, died in 1937, three years after their golden wedding anniversary.

NORMAN BRUCE REAM (1844 -1915), financier. Ream volunteered at seventeen for the Union Army and was active in many battles until he was severely wounded in Georgia in 1864. After recuperation he returned to the front and was wounded in each succeeding battle in which he participated, until he resigned due to complete incapacitation. He invested heavily in Chicago railroads and real estate and acted as broker for the Armour meatpacking concern in 1879, buying pork at six dollars a barrel and selling it at nineteen. Ream was a close friend and business associate of George Pullman and of JIC member Marshall Field. He was a leader of the "Big Four" of the Chicago Board of Trade, who buoyed the market in the 1883 crash. In 1888 he moved from Chicago to New York City and became a member of the Stock Exchange as well as a director of twenty-two corporations. Ream was one of the organizers and a director of both the National Biscuit Company and U. S. Steel. He financed the building of Chicago's first skyscraper, the Rookery. Robert Todd Lincoln, son of President Lincoln, served as a pall bearer at his funeral. Ream left the bulk of his $40 million estate to his wife, Carrie Putnam, who died in 1924.

LANSING PARMALEE REED (1882 - 1937), attorney. He was a partner at the New York law firm of Davis, Polk, Wardwell, Gardiner & Reed as well as a director of IT&T and of Guaranty Trust

Company of New York. One of his law partners was John W. Davis, Democratic nominee for U. S. President. Reed's clients included J.P. Morgan & Company, IT&T, Guaranty Trust, Morgan Stanley, and Brown Harriman Company. Reed, a son of the Rev. Dr. Edward A. Reed, of Springfield, Massachusetts, married Ruth Lawrence, a daughter of the Right Rev. William Lawrence, the Episcopal Bishop of Massachusetts from 1893 to 1925, who was known as "the banker Bishop" because his fund raising drives "invariably developed with Midas-like magic." Mrs. Reed's two brothers, William Appleton Lawrence and Frederic Lawrence of Boston, also became bishops.

JAMES RENWICK, JR. (1818 -1895), architect. Renwick entered Columbia College (now University) at the age of twelve, graduated in 1836, and received a master of arts degree three years later. In 1861 he married Anna Lloyd Aspinwall, who was a sister and aunt of JIC members. Renwick designed several well-known New York City churches, including Grace Episcopal, St. Bartholomew's, and St. Patrick's Cathedral, and was the architect for Washington's Smithsonian Institution. His other designs included Vassar College and a new façade for the New York Stock Exchange. He also designed Washington's first Corcoran Gallery of Art, now known as the Renwick. He and his wife, who had no children, were art collectors. His finest achievement, St. Patrick's Cathedral in New York City, began work in 1858, was interrupted by the War, and opened in May of 1879. The archbishops of New York are buried there under the high altar.

WILLIAM KING RICHARDSON (1859 -1951), attorney. He was a partner in the Boston law firm of Fish, Richardson & Neave,

Renwick's Smithsonian Institution in Washington, D. C.

specializing in patent law. Richardson represented Bell Telephone in its early patent litigation. He retired from practice in 1927 and, unmarried, devoted himself to book collecting. His extensive collection was left to his alma mater, Harvard, and is now housed in the Richardson Room of the Houghton Library.

FRANCIS GEORGE BURKE-ROCHE (1885-1958). His grandfather, Frank Work, grew up in Ohio with few resources and left for New York City while still in his teens. There he contrived an "accidental" meeting with Commodore Vanderbilt and began as his protégé, ending as his stock broker. By the time of his death he had accumulated a fortune of $17 million. One of Work's daughters married New York's socially prominent Peter Cooper Hewitt, who invented the mercury vapor lamp and obtained the first patents for a working helicopter. Work's other daughter, Frances, married in 1880 against her father's wishes James Boothby Burke-Roche, an almost penniless young Irishman from a recently ennobled family (but her father did pay the groom's $50,000 gambling debts). By the time of their divorce in 1891 they had two daughters and twin sons, Edmund and Francis, the latter named for his mother and grandfather. As a condition to sharing his wealth, Frank Work demanded that his grandchildren be reared in America and have nothing to do with their father's family. In 1905 Frances married Hungarian horse trainer Aurel Batonyi and her father completely cut her out of his will and denied her generous financial stipend. After the marriage was annulled she was restored to her father's favor. Three months before the death in 1920 of Frances' ex-husband, he succeeded as the 3rd Baron Fermoy and

the elder of her twin sons was the heir presumptive to the Barony. By that time Frank Work was dead but his twin grandsons were far more American than British. JIC member Francis graduated from Harvard in 1908 and served in the U. S. Navy during World War I, thus acquiring U. S. citizenship even though he was born in London. He managed the Paris branch of Guaranty Trust Company for twenty years, spending his summers in Newport. While living in France he was president of the Paris Harvard Club while his twin brother was president of the London Harvard Club. His twin, Edmund, succeeded their father as the 4th Baron Fermoy. His daughter, Frances (named for her American grandmother) married the eventual 8th Earl Spencer. Their daughter, Diana Frances, married the Prince of Wales, heir to the British throne. Prince Charles' heirs, Princes William and Harry, thus boast a prominent American heritage. JIC member Francis Burke-Roche never married and was survived by his sister, Cynthia, wife of Guy Fairfax Cary, whose grandfather was the powerful Episcopal Bishop Potter of New York. Cynthia lived at Elm Court, their family's Newport summer estate.

WILLIAM ROCKEFELLER (1841-1922), capitalist and oil executive. The younger brother of John D. Rockefeller, in 1865 he joined his brother in the oil business and established a branch in New York City known as Rockefeller & Company. In that year they built the Standard Oil Works in Cleveland, Ohio, and the following year Henry M. Flagler became their partner. The Standard Oil Company of Ohio was formed in 1870 with John D. as president and William as Vice President. In 1881 the Standard Oil Trust

Left: Frances Burke-Roche, whose elder twin son succeeded as the 4th Baron Fermoy while the younger twin, Francis (named for her and for her father), was a Jekyll member. Mrs. Burke-Roche's granddaughter, Frances, was named for her and gave her own daughter the name Diana Frances. She was to become among the best-known women in the world as Diana, Princess of Wales.

Right: The handsome Burke-Roche twins, Edmund and Francis. Edmund's great-grandson, Prince William, is heir apparent to his father, the Prince of Wales.

Above: The oil tanker William Rockefeller, sunk off the coast of Cape Hatteras, North Carolina, by the German submarine U-701 on June 28, 1942, losing 136,000 barrels of oil.

Far left: William Rockefeller with one of his grandsons.

Left: William Rockefeller at Jekyll Island.

was formed and capitalized at $95 million when the Standard Oil Company of New York was established with William Rockefeller as its president, a position he retained until 1911. He was also a director of the Delaware, Lackawanna and Western Railroad as well as other corporations. In 1913 Rockefeller testified before the U. S. Senate's Pujo Committee at his Jekyll apartment at "Sans Souci" but the hearing was quickly cancelled within minutes due to his fit of coughing. In 1886, William Rockefeller became interested in property along the Hudson River owned by JIC member General Lloyd Aspinwall and purchased it for $150,000. He turned Rockwood into the most magnificent mansion along the Hudson, using the estate as a summer residence, renaming it Rockwood Hall, and eventually began living there year round. Rockefeller married in 1864 Almira "Mira" Goodsell, sister of Mrs. Oliver Jennings (thus a close family relation of the Auchincloss, Brewster, Coe, James, Jennings and Brown families at Jekyll). He purchased in 1905 Indian Mound Cottage at Jekyll and made extensive additions and renovations as his family's use increased over the years. He also purchased a fifty-thousand-acre preserve in the Adirondacks with a family lodge and necessary supporting buildings and staff. The Rockefeller children were Emma, who married David McAlpin; William Goodsell, who married Elsie Stillman; Percy Avery, who married Isabel Stillman (sister of Elsie); and Ethel Geraldine who married Marcellus Hartley Dodge, nephew of JIC member Helen Hartley Jenkins who reared him after the death of his mother during childbirth. The Stillman sisters were daughters of JIC member James Stillman, president and chairman of National City Bank. Almira Rockefeller died of heart failure at Indian Mound, their Jekyll Island home, in 1920, but her husband continued to winter there in his succeeding two years. William and Elsie Rockefeller's son, James Stillman Rockefeller, was, at his death at 102, the oldest living Olympic gold medalist (for rowing at the 1924 Paris games) in the world. He married Nancy Carnegie, grand-niece of Andrew Carnegie, whose family owned Cumberland Island near Jekyll. After Rockefeller's death his Jekyll home, Indian Mound Cottage, was sold to his son-in-law's aunt and substitute mother, JIC member Helen Hartley Jenkins.

EDMUND PENDLETON ROGERS (1882-1966), sportsman. His first wife was Edith Elliott, who died in childbirth at home in 1919 at the birth of her second son. Rogers then married in 1931 Dorothy Knox Goodyear, the widow of JIC member Frank Henry Goodyear, Jr., who was killed in an auto accident. The next year Rogers became a JIC member. His brother, Herman, was a close friend of Wallis Simpson prior to her relationship with Britain's King Edward VIII. When the then-King determined to abdicate the throne and marry Wallis, he had Herman Rogers call his brother, JIC member Edmund, to ask about the advisability of having the marriage occur in France at the Château de Candé. The 1937 marriage took place with Herman Rogers giving away the bride and his wife, Katherine, as part of the small party. In 1939 Mr. and Mrs. Edmund P. Rogers purchased in Aiken, South Carolina, "Rye Patch," a ten-acre estate adjoining Hopelands Gardens. They added a wing, developed gardens, and entertained the Duke and Duchess of Windsor there. After Mrs. Rogers' death in 1984, her children gave the estate to the City of Aiken. Edmund P. Rogers, his first wife, and their sons are buried in St. James Cemetery in Hyde Park, New York.

FAIRMAN ROGERS (1833 -1900), civil engineer. Rogers was professor of civil engineering at the University of Pennsylvania and one of the original members of the National Academy of Sciences. Author of *The Magnetism of Iron Vessels,* in 1862 he completed the survey of the Potomac River northward from Blakiston Island. Rogers acted as manager of the Pennsylvania Academy of Fine Arts and was one of the first to introduce polo into the United States. In 1879 Thomas Eakins painted *May Morning in the Park* which was a portrait of Fairman Rogers (who wrote *A Manual of Coaching* in 1901). The painting is now known as *Fairman Rogers Four-in-Hand.* His sister's son, Walter Rogers Furness, was a JIC member.

DEXTER PHELPS RUMSEY (1828-1906), banker and merchant. With his brother, Bronson, they were members of the firm of A. Rumsey & Company founded by their father. They sold their father's tannery business and invested the $10 million each they received in railroads and real estate. At one time they owned twenty-two of Buffalo's forty-three square miles. Dexter Rumsey was married three times and had children by his first and third marriages. In 1878 he purchased a home in Buffalo as a gift to his daughter, Cornelia, upon her marriage to Ansley Wilcox, a Buffalo lawyer. After her death, Wilcox married her sister, Mary Grace, and the house was in turn given to them. When President McKinley was assassinated in Buffalo in 1901, Theodore Roosevelt was sworn in as president in the library of the Ansley Wilcox home. Dexter

Rumsey's daughter by his third wife (who was thirty years younger than he), Ruth, married William "Wild Bill" Donovan, head of the Office of Strategic Services which became the Central Intelligence Agency of the United States.

CHARLES E. SAMPSON (1856 -1946), broker. He was a commission merchant broker at the firm started by his father, O. H. Sampson & Company of Boston. He moved to New York City in 1900 and joined Catlin & Company. For many years Sampson was a trustee of the Cathedral of St. John the Divine in New York City. He and his family also had a home at Tuxedo Park. A fund left in his will enabled purchases for the Metropolitan Museum of Art.

GRANGE SARD (1843- 1924), manufacturer. Sard was chairman of the board of Rathbone, Sard & Company, stove manufacturers. He was also president of the Union Trust Company of Albany. He married Caroline S. Woolverton in 1870 and they lived both in Albany and Southampton. One of their daughters married sugar heir Heber R. Bishop.

JAMES DENISON SAWYER (JIC member 1930-31; died 1943), broker. An 1896 graduate of Yale, Sawyer was a partner at Eastman, Dillon & Company. In 1925 he married Ethel Cochrane Cushing, widow of artist Howard Gardner Cushing and daughter of JIC member Alexander Cochrane. Her son by her first marriage, Alexander Cochrane Cushing, founded Squaw Valley and successfully located the 1960 winter Olympics there. Her granddaughter, Lily Dulany Emmet, married Anthony West, son of H. G. Wells and Rebecca West.

GRANT BARNEY SCHLEY (1845 - 1917), broker. He was the

President Taft and Secretary Knox at the Buffalo home of Ansley Wilcox, a gift to his daughter from Dexter Rumsey. Theodore Roosevelt was sworn in here as president after McKinley's assassination.

senior partner at the brokerage/banking firm of Moore & Schley, co-founded in 1885 by Schley and banker John G. Moore. Schley was a self-made man with an elementary school education. He had innate mathematical ability and worked his way up through American Express, then to First National Bank, where he became head of the bank's foreign exchange department and married the bank director's daughter, Elizabeth Baker (only sister of JIC member George F. Baker) in 1879. A member of the New York Stock Exchange, his clients included Henry H. Rogers, William C. Whitney, Thomas F. Ryan, JIC member William Rockefeller, and Oliver H. Payne. He served as chairman of the board of the Underwood Typewriter Company, president of a number of mining companies and as a director of several corporations. Moore & Schley was involved in the deal forming the American Tobacco Company in 1900. After the Bank Panic of 1907, Moore & Schley was left with a $25 million debt and was among the firms saved from failure by a trust company bailout orchestrated by JIC member J.P. Morgan. In 1975, the company, then a New York-based regional broker, merged with du Pasquier & Company and was sold by them in 1989. In 1887, Schley and his wife traveled by horse-drawn carriage to visit a friend in rural New Jersey. She is said to have exclaimed on the beautiful vista of "far hills," thus giving name to the place where there was not yet a village. They both liked the area so much that they bought fifteen hundred acres on the North Branch, including the hills, which since have been known as Schley Mountain. On the knoll above the river the Schleys built "Froh-Heim," a rambling country house with Japanese accents, and all its required service buildings.

GUSTAV HENRY SCHWAB (1851 -1912), importer and steamship agent. Schwab was a member of the shipping merchant firm of Oelrichs & Company. At his father's death in 1888 he assumed leadership of the American office of the North German Lloyd Steamship Company. He was a director of several corporations and was decorated by the Italian King and by the German emperor. A founder of the Provident Loan Society of New York, he lived in what is now the University Heights area of Brooklyn. Schwab married in 1876 Caroline Wheeler and they had a son and a daughter.

JAMES ALEXANDER SCRYMSER (1839 -1918), cable executive. Founder of the All America cable system, Scrymser was president of the Central and South American Cable Company as well as the Mexican Telegraph Company. He went to his friend and fellow JIC member Alfred Pell with the idea of joining the U. S. by cable with Cuba and secured the financial backing from Moses Taylor and money from Morgan Drexel. After his initial company was successful, he sold it to Jay Gould, took the proceeds and connected the U. S. to Mexico and to Central and South America by cable. In 1917 he became the first person to establish a telegraph line between the U. S. and Brazil. Scrymser asked JIC member John Kennedy Stewart to give the money to build the United Charities Building in New York City. He gave $1 million to American Red Cross to build their headquarters building in Washington, D.C. in 1911. Scrymser married in 1868 Mary C. Prime and they had no children. He broke his hip three years before his death and moved to Jekyll Island to recuperate; he had just returned to New York City when he died.

HENRY FRANCIS SEARS (1862 - 1942), physician. Sears graduated from Harvard in 1883 then attended Harvard law School for one year before transferring to its medical school where he graduated in 1887 and received a masters degree in 1888. He was a pathologist at Boston City Hospital from 1888 until 1894 when he retired from practice. He married in 1904 at Geneva, Switzerland, Jean Struthers, daughter of JIC member William Struthers, and had three children. They lived in the Sears town house on Beacon Hill and at their summer house in Beverly. His daughter, Emily, married U. S. Senator and Ambassador Henry Cabot Lodge, the Republican vice-presidential nominee in 1960 with Richard Nixon. Sears' son, Henry, revived the America's Cup race after a twenty-one-year lapse and was a commodore of the New York Yacht Club.

FREDERICK CHEEVER SHATTUCK (1847 -1929), physician. Shattuck served his alma mater, Harvard, as an overseer and was president of the board and a Fellow of the American Academy of Arts and Sciences. In retirement he was a professor emeritus of Harvard Medical School to whom he was a generous contributor. Shattuck and his wife, Elizabeth Lee, had two sons and two daughters.

EDWIN BERNON SHELDON (JIC member 1901-1907). He and his wife lived in New York City and at "Longwood" near Delhi, New York, which was razed in 1938 to build a school. His wife was a daughter of Henry J. Whitehouse, second Episcopal bishop of Illinois. Mrs. Sheldon's nephew, William Fitzhugh Whitehouse, married Frances Sheldon and they were the parents of Lily

Whitehouse who married Colonel Charles Coventry, son of the 9th Earl of Coventry. Lily's youngest son succeeded as the 12th Earl of Coventry but died without a son. Lily's daughter, Pamela, married the 9th Earl of Ayelsford. Sheldon was a family relation of JIC member Bernon Sheldon Prentice.

GEORGE FREDERICK SHRADY (1837 -1907), physician. Shrady was acting assistant surgeon of the U. S. Army during the Civil War and attended President U. S. Grant during his final illness. He was a prominent author on medical matters and advised the doctors caring for the dying Emperor Frederick of Prussia, son-in-law of Queen Victoria, during the final weeks before his death. In 1890 he was one of the physicians appointed to attend the electrocution of the first person sentenced to die by that method and, as a result, Shrady became a vocal critic of the procedure. After President Garfield's assassination, Shrady was consulted as a surgical pathologist and reported to the medical profession and the public on the results of the autopsy. He also took part in the autopsy on the body of Garfield's assassin, Charles Guiteau. Shrady was secretary and then president of the New York Pathological Society, a manager of the Hudson River Hospital for the Insane, a trustee of the Hudson State Hospital for the Insane at Poughkeepsie, and for many years served on the editorial staff of the *New York Herald.* He first married in 1860 Mary Lewis, who died in 1883 having had three sons and a daughter. Five years later he married the widowed Hester E. Cantine who had a daughter, Sarah, whom Shrady adopted. Sarah was the wife of JIC member Edwin Gould, who nominated his father-in-law for membership and began the process to build the Shrady's Jekyll

Steamship agent Gustav Schwab in his New York office.

home in 1904. In 1902, Shrady's son, Henry Merwin Shrady, was chosen as the sculptor for the statue of President Grant astride a horse in the nation's capital.

HESTER ELLEN CANTINE SHRADY (Mrs. George Frederick Shrady) (JIC member 1908-1916). She was a widow with one daughter when she married Dr. George Shrady in 1888. After her husband's death she became a member in her own right and continued to use their Jekyll home to entertain family and friends. In 1917 her eldest grandson, Edwin Gould, Jr., died in a hunting accident at Jekyll and she did not return to the Island for four years. Her daughter, however, mother of the boy who was killed, never returned to Jekyll. In 1925 she sold her home there to Club president Dr. Walter B. James, who renamed it "Cherokee."

GEORGE THERON SLADE (1872-1941), railway executive. Born in New York City and educated at Yale where he was a classmate of Louis Hill, son of JIC member James J. Hill, Slade married in 1901 Charlotte, daughter of the senior Hill. He was president of the Absaroka Oil Development Company as well as the Tide Water Oil Company. In 1903 he was President of the Erie Railway when James J. Hill brought him to the Great Northern Railway. Slade moved to the Northern Pacific Railway, also controlled by Hill, in 1910. In 1918 he resigned his position and volunteered to become director of transportation for the American Expeditionary Forces in France. After the War he returned to the Northern Pacific Railway. The Slades lived in St. Paul until after his wife's death in 1923 at the age of forty-eight; then he moved to New York City and lived in quiet retirement. They had a son and

a daughter.

JOHN SLOANE (1834- 1905), rug merchant. Born in Scotland, he was a partner of his brothers Henry T. and William D. Sloane (the latter of whom married Emily Vanderbilt). Sloane was president of W. & J. Sloane Co. from 1891 until his death. He opened offices around the world and won the contract for all the carpeting for the coronation of Nicholas II of Russia. He married in 1867 Adela Berry, who died in 1911. They lived in a Fifth Avenue mansion and at "Wyndhurst," their estate near Lenox, Massachusetts, with a stable of driving horses. Wyndhurst was a Tudor-style cottage on 380 acres with grounds designed by Frederick Law Olmsted. It is now an exclusive spa and golf course. Sloane's granddaughter, Grace Sloane, married U. S. Secretary of State Cyrus Vance, while his niece married JIC member John Henry Hammond.

JOHN SLOANE, JR. (1883-1971), rug merchant. A son of JIC member John Sloane, he was chairman of the board and a director of W. & J. Sloane Company. He married Elsie Nicoll in 1917. During World War II she was chairman of the U. N. Officers Club under the auspices of the English-Speaking Union. Among their three daughters was Mrs. Cyrus Vance.

JAMES HOPKINS SMITH (JIC member 1897-1900). Smith, a native of Portland, Maine, was an officer of U. S. Bank. In 1884 he built "Stonecroft," a shingle style summer cottage in Portland which was later to become the Payson Estate. His son, James Hopkins Smith, Jr., married Pauline Morton, a leader of the movement to repeal the eighteenth amendment. Her grandfather, J. Sterling

George T. Slade was a Yale classmate of James J. Hill's son. He married Hill's daughter and was hired by his father-in-law to join the family's railroads.

Charlotte Hill Slade, whose father, mother, husband, sister, and five brothers-in-law were Jekyll members.

Morton, was United States secretary of agriculture as well as senator and governor of Nebraska. Her father, a railroad executive and later president of the Equitable Life Assurance Society, served as secretary of the navy from 1904 to 1905. Her uncle founded Morton Salt and she inherited several million dollars from the family fortune. She and her husband had two sons, Paul Morton and James Hopkins, the latter of whom became assistant secretary of the navy for air. At the beginning of World War I, after her husband left to serve in the French ambulance corps, Pauline Smith obtained a divorce and began an interior decorating business. In 1916 she married recently divorced Charles H. Sabin, president of Guaranty Trust Company of New York.

ROBERT DICKSON SMITH (JIC member 1886-1888; died 1888), attorney. Smith graduated from Harvard in 1857 and received his law degree there in 1860. He practiced law in Suffolk County, Massachusetts, and served as an overseer of Harvard from 1878 until his death.

FREDERICK AUGUSTUS SNOW (JIC member 1915-1918; rejoined 1925-1929), real estate. He invested heavily in real estate which he managed through his firm, Snow and Snow. He and his wife, formerly Mary Palen, lived in New York City and at Southampton. They had a son, George Palen Snow, whose wife, Carmel Snow, was the well-known editor-in-chief of *Harper's Bazaar* from 1934-1958. She launched the careers of many of the day's fashion giants and championed her concept of "well-dressed women with well-dressed minds."

LOUISA VIVIAN BENNING SPENCER (Mrs. Samuel

Spencer) (JIC member from 1909; died 1919). She was a daughter of H. L. Benning, Georgia Supreme Court Justice, for whom Fort Benning is named. She married in 1872 Samuel Spencer, president of the Southern Railway, who was killed in a wreck on his railroad line near Lynchburg, Virginia, in 1906. He left an estate of more than $2 million. Mrs. Spencer lived in Washington, D.C. and at "Cragsworth" in Tuxedo Park where she died in 1919.

SAMUEL SPENCER (1847 -1906), railway president. Born in Columbus, Georgia, Spencer volunteered for the Confederate Army before graduating from the University of Georgia and the University of Virginia. He married in 1872 Louisa Benning. Spencer was president of the B & O Railroad and a director of several others, including the Central of Georgia. In 1889 he became affiliated with the banking house of Drexel, Morgan & Company as their railroad expert, eventually becoming a partner at Morgan's company. In 1894 he became president of the Southern Railway Company. On Thanksgiving Day, 1906, Spencer was traveling on his railroad to North Carolina for a hunting trip when he was killed in a train wreck near Lynchburg, Virginia. He and his family lived in New York City at "Cragsworth" in Tuxedo Park, New York. His granddaughter, Agnes Layng, married Ashbel Green, secretary of the New York Stock Exchange.

JOHN ALDEN SPOOR (1851 – 1926), capitalist. Born in New York, Spoor moved to Chicago as a young man. He was president and chairman of the board of Chicago Junction Railway Company and of Union Stock Yard & Transit Company. A member of the Chicago stock exchange, he served as a director of several corporations. In

Jekyll member George F. Baker, whose grandson, George Baker St. George, was also a Jekyll member. St. George's wife served 18 years in Congress.

1905 he bought "Blythewood Farms," a 470-acre estate home in the Berkshires near Pittsfield, Massachusetts, which had belonged to the widow of Wirt Dexter Walker, nephew and namesake of JIC member Wirt Dexter. Under the terms of her late husband's will, Mrs. Walker forfeited the house upon her remarriage. Spoor married in 1889 Frances Samuel of St. Louis, and they became benefactors of St.

Chrystostom's Episcopal Church in Chicago.

GEORGE BAKER ST. GEORGE (1892 - 1957), sportsman and bank director. A grandson of JIC member George F. Baker for whom he was named (his mother, Eva, was Baker's eldest child), St. George graduated from Cambridge. He was reared at several homes in England, including an art-filled house in London his mother inherited from her father in addition to $5 million. St. George was one of England's leading racquets players. He was a director of his grandfather's First National Bank and president of the St. George Coal Company. St. George married in 1917 Katharine Delano P. Collier and thereafter lived in New York City and Tuxedo Park. Katharine Collier St. George was a Republican congresswoman from New York who was born in England but came to the U.S. at the age of two. She was elected to Congress in 1946, served until 1964, and died in 1983. The St. George's daughter, Priscilla, married Angier Biddle Duke. George St. George's sister, Evelyn (called "Gardenia"), married Sir Derrick Gunston, Baronet, while their niece, Diana, married Sir George Earle, Baronet.

JOSEPH LEWIS STACKPOLE (1838-1904), attorney. Stackpole graduated from Harvard in 1859, then entered military services as a brevet lieutenant colonel of volunteers in the Union army. After the War he practiced law in Massachusetts then became a judge. His father, also a Harvard graduate, was killed in a railroad accident in 1847. His mother's sister was married to John Lothrop Motley, U. S. Ambassador to Austria and to Great Britain.

JOHN STEWARD (1847-1923), broker. A member of the New York Stock Exchange, Steward lived in Goshen, New York. He graduated from Columbia in 1868, and in 1871 he married Cordelia Schermerhorn Jones, a niece of "the" Mrs. Astor. They spent much of their married life in England where U. S. Ambassador Henry White, Steward's cousin (their grandfathers were brothers who married sisters), often stayed with them in Leicestershire. Steward left Goshen, New York, in his private railway car en route to California and died in Rawlins, Wyoming.

GEORGE DAVID STEWART (1862 -1933), surgeon and medical professor. Born in Nova Scotia, Stewart graduated from New York University and became a professor and head of the department of surgery at Bellevue Hospital in New York. He was a close friend and personal physician of JIC member George F. Baker who gave $1 million to NYU Hospital in his honor. Stewart was a founder of the American College of Surgeons and enjoyed a reputation as a great after-dinner speaker (of prohibition, he said, "Russia went dry in 1915 and then went crazy in 1917"). He was a close friend and personal physician of JIC member James J. Hill. He married Ida M. Robb in 1890 and one of their daughters married Edward Hope Coffey, Jr. who wrote *She Loves Me Not* under the pseudonym Edward Hope. He adapted his novel for the 1934 movie starring Bing Crosby.

JOHN AIKMAN STEWART (1822 - 1926), banker. A native New Yorker who was called "the dean of American bankers," and died at the age of 103, Stewart recalled having watched the great fire of 1835 that almost destroyed New York City. In 1853 when he was an actuary for the U.S. Life Insurance Company of New York, Stewart petitioned the New York State legislature to approve the creation of a financial company in New York City that would act as executor and trustee for the funds of individuals and institutions. Stewart, who was Lincoln's assistant treasurer of the U.S. during part of the Civil War (he dined with Lincoln at the White House just days before the assassination), would serve U.S. Trust for 73 years—as secretary, president, and chairman of the board. Stewart was also financial advisor to Presidents Lincoln and Grover Cleveland and served as acting president of Princeton from 1910 to 1912 when Woodrow Wilson left to become governor. Incongruously for such a capitalist, his granddaughter, Frances Violet Stewart, was married to Norman M. Thomas, six times Socialist candidate for president of the U.S., whom she met at a tuberculosis clinic where she was a social worker. They lived in an apartment in a crowded tenement district where he was doing social work for Christ Church while attending Union Theological Seminary. Stewart's grandson, William Adams Walker Stewart, was also a JIC member.

WILLIAM ADAMS WALKER STEWART (1876 -1960), attorney. A grandson of JIC member John Aikman Stewart, his father was lost on the yacht Cythera in the West Indies in March 1888, along with the father of JIC member Cornelius Smith Lee. A Princeton and Columbia graduate, Stewart was a member of the law firm of Stewart & Shearer which merged into Carter, Ledyard & Milburn in 1952. He was commodore of the New York Yacht Club and president of the Bar Association of New York 1930-31 as well as a trustee of the U. S. Trust Company. In 1900 he married Frances DeForest, daughter of JIC member Robert DeForest. They had four daughters and two sons.

CAROLYN "CARRIE" FOSTER STICKNEY (Mrs. Joseph Stickney) (1869-1936). A daughter of Reuben Foster, a Boston commission merchant, she married in 1893 railroad owner Joseph Stickney. Ten years after her husband's death she married Aymon, Prince Faucigny Lucinge (1862- 1922), a descendant of King Charles X of France. She owned hotels in France and Switzerland and continued to operate the Mt. Washington Hotel, which she visited every year, until her death. Her nephew, Foster Stickney, inherited the hotel from her and ran it for ten years before selling to a Boston syndicate in 1944. In that year the hotel was used for an international meeting of financiers from forty-four countries known as the Bretton Woods International Monetary Conference where the World Bank and the International Monetary Fund were organized and the American dollar designated as the standard of international exchange.

JOSEPH STICKNEY (JIC member 1886-1903; died 1903), coal and railroad owner. A native of Concord, New Hampshire, Stickney owned a Pennsylvania anthracite coal firm and railroad. In 1881 he purchased Mount Pleasant House and ten thousand acres of land in New Hampshire in view of Mt. Washington, later called Bretton Woods. He then used two million board feet of lumber and employed 250 Italian artisans to build the Mount Washington Hotel. At its lavish opening in 1902, he exclaimed, "Look at me, gentlemen, for I am the poor fool who built all this." Within eighteen months he was dead and his widow, Carolyn, inherited the hotel and his fortune. She built the Stickney Memorial Chapel in his memory and in 1910 the Bretton Woods Boy Singers were organized to serve as the choir for the Chapel. A disagreement concerning Stickney's will, with his widow as executrix, was litigated all the way to the U. S. Supreme

Court five years after his death.

JAMES STILLMAN (1850 – 1918), banker. Born in Texas, he began as a partner in Woodward and Stillman, cotton merchants. He succeeded JIC member Percy R. Pyne, son-in-law of Stillman's mentor, Moses Taylor, as president of National City Bank (which eventually became Citicorp), a position he held from 1891 until 1909 when he became chairman of the board. Stillman also served on several corporate boards including Western Union and the C&N Railroad. Among his most valued clients was Standard Oil because he held large cash reserves favored by JIC member William Rockefeller and thus his bank had cash when others did not. Of the "Big Three" U. S. bankers, Stillman, J. P. Morgan, and George F. Baker, all were JIC members. They personally intervened in the nation's financial crisis of 1907 to prevent massive bankruptcies of the nation's financial institutions. Although called before the U. S. Senate's Pujo Committee to testify about a supposed "money trust" that ran the country, Stillman was in Europe and was not forced to return for an appearance. In 1910 Stillman assisted in arranging secret meetings at Jekyll Island that resulted in establishing the forerunner of the Federal Reserve System. When World War I broke out, Stillman donated his home in Paris to the French government for use as a hospital and contributed large sums of money to war victims. He married Elizabeth Rumrill although she spent the last decades of her life in Europe and did not see her husband or children during all that time. Two of their daughters married sons of JIC member William Rockefeller. He gave the Stillman Infirmary to Harvard, and two of his pallbearers were JIC members J. P. Morgan

Josephine Stickney costumed for a ball. Ten years after the death of her husband, she married Prince Aymon Faucingy-Lucigne. They lived in France and Switzerland but every year visited her hotel in New Hampshire.

Edward Stotesbury, "the richest man at Morgan's," whose annual income exceeded five million dollars.

and John A. Stewart.

EDWARD TOWNSEND STOTESBURY (1849 – 1938), banker. He was the resident senior partner at Drexel & Company, the premier banking house in Philadelphia, where he was born. Stotesbury then became the senior partner at J. P. Morgan where by 1919 his income was $5,585,000 and, in 1927, he was known as "the richest man at Morgan's." Reaching an eventual net worth of $100 million, he was asked his advice about success and replied, "Keep your mouth shut and your ears open." Stotesbury was a director of many railroads and corporations and was decorated by France and Italy. He lived at "Whitemarsh Hall" in Chestnut Hill, Pennsylvania, and raised thoroughbred horses at his farm, "Wingo." He was the American representative to the International Horse Show at the London Olympic Meet in 1908 and, in the next year, personally assumed the entire indebtedness of the Philadelphia Grand Opera Company. "Whitemarsh Hall" was called "America's Versailles" requiring a staff of 150 and in 1929, $1 million for annual upkeep. Built on six floors, three of which were below ground to achieve symmetry, the house contained 147 rooms, forty-five bathrooms, three elevators, a sixty-four-foot-long ballroom, and an organ with three-story pipes. President Taft attended his second marriage to Eva Cromwell on whom he reportedly settled $4 million. Eva preferred "El Mirasol," their home in Palm Beach, where she achieved her objective to become queen of society. Stotesbury withdrew $55 million from his account at Morgan's between 1933 and his death – a rate of withdrawal of more than $10 million a year. His stepson, James H.R. Cromwell (one-time U. S. Minister to Canada), who was then married to Doris Duke, had become a devoted New Dealer. One day in 1936 Stotesbury told him, "It's a good thing you married the richest girl in the world because you will get very little from me. I made my fortune and I am going to squander it myself; not your friend Roosevelt." Almost $9 million was left in his estate after his death. Stotesbury's step-daughter was successively the wife of Gen. Douglas McArthur and actor Lionel Atwill.

RALPH BEAVER STRASSBURGER (1883 – 1959), publisher and diplomat. A Naval Academy graduate, Strassburger was publisher of the Norristown Times and a breeder of thoroughbred and hunting horses. He married in 1911 May Bourne, daughter of JIC member Frederick G. Bourne, president of the Singer Sewing Machine Company. He was appointed in 1913 by President Taft to be counsel general and secretary of the legation to Romania, Bulgaria, and Serbia, and was later secretary of the legation to Tokyo. Strassburger was an unsuccessful candidate for U. S. Congress in 1914. He owned racing stables in the U.S., France, England, and Ireland, and was decorated by the government of France. In 1924 Strassburger purchased a chateau at Deauville built by Baron Henri de Rothschild in 1907 on land which had been the home of Gustave Flaubert. The Strassburgers furnished it lavishly and in 1980 their son gave it to the town of Deauville. The Strassburgers owned several homes: "Normandy Farm" in Gwynedd Valley, Pennsylvania; a villa in Paris; "La Ferme du Coteau" in Deauville, France; and "Villa Pennsylvanie" in Chantilly, France. In 1919 he purchased the Fairbank-Ferguson Cottage at Jekyll Island but sold it in 1923 to his sister-in-law, Marjorie Bourne Thayer. He wrote two books: a

Above: Stotesbury's Whitemarsh Hall near Philadelphia. The annual bill for maintenance was more than one million dollars to sustain a staff of 150.

Right: Ralph Beaver Strassburger, publisher and diplomat.

genealogy of the Strassburger family, and one on German settlers in Pennsylvania. In addition to her father, Mrs. Strassburger's sisters, Marjorie and Marion Bourne, were JIC members, as were her brothers-in-law, Alexander Dallas Thayer and Robert George Elbert.

WILLIAM STRUTHERS (1848-1911), marble manufacturer. In partnership with his brother, John, Struthers owned a Philadelphia marble works business. Their grandfather, who founded the firm, designed and installed at his own expense the marble vault for George Washington's grave at Mt. Vernon. Their sister, Helen, was married to JIC member Rudolph Ellis. In 1896 Struthers constructed Moss Cottage, the first at Jekyll to be wired for electricity. During the 1900 Christmas season he was the first to bring an automobile to Jekyll but, because of the noise it generated, he was asked to return it to Philadelphia. Struthers retired from his business when young and moved his family to "Woodlea," an estate he built near Bryn Mawr, Pennsylvania. He married in 1870 Savannah "Vannie" Durburrow, who had been born in Georgia but reared in Philadelphia. Their daughter, Jean, married in 1904 in Switzerland JIC member Henry Francis Sears with artist Mary Cassatt in attendance. The Sears' daughter, Emily, was one of only two Jekyll member babies to be christened at Faith Chapel. She was to marry Henry Cabot Lodge, U. S. senator, ambassador, and Richard Nixon's vice-presidential running mate in 1960.

EDWARD TAYLOR HUNT TALMAGE (1867 - 1922), broker and coachman. A member of the New York Stock Exchange, Talmage retired from business in 1912 and lived in New York City and Bernardsville, New Jersey. He was a member of the Union Club, the Racquet and Tennis Club, and Sons of the American Revolution, and was also active in coaching. He married Mary Prentice and had a son and daughter.

WILLIAM HICKOK TAYLOR (1858-1914), railroad executive. Taylor was first vice president of the St. Louis Southwestern Railway and a director and executive committee member of the Equitable Trust Company. He graduated from Columbia and lived in New York City. Taylor married Eleanore Simmons in 1901; his fellow JIC member Edwin Gould was an usher at the wedding. He was survived by his wife, mother, and four brothers.

JOHN TAYLOR TERRY, JR. (1857- 1942), attorney. Terry's father was a partner and chairman of E. D. Morgan bankers. The son graduated from Yale and Columbia and studied at the University of Bonn in Germany. He began practicing law in New York in 1881 and was a bank trustee. He married Bertha Halsted in 1885 and had a son and a daughter. Terry's brother was clergyman Roderick Terry, president of the Newport Historical Society and Redwood Library, whose wife inherited a Newport mansion from her father, New York art collector Henry Marquand. Roderick Terry was a bibliophile who collected all the autographs of the signers of the Constitution as well as Washington Irving memorabilia.

ALEXANDER DALLAS THAYER (1888 - 1968), sportsman and yachtsman. The son of Brig. Gen. Russell Thayer, young Thayer was an outstanding athlete at the University of Pennsylvania where

Left: A hunting party at Jekyll given by the Struthers family.

Above: The taxidermy shop at Jekyll was among the Club's busiest services.

The grand trotter Edwin Thorne by Thornedale.

he graduated in 1910. In 1908 he was the men's doubles tennis national champion. He was a pilot in World War I and in 1926 married Marjorie Bourne, a daughter of JIC member Frederick G. Bourne, president of the Singer Sewing Machine Company. They lived at her Gwynllan Farm near her parents' estate. In 1923 she had purchased her father's former cottage at Jekyll Island. In 1928 the Thayers commissioned to be built in Germany a steel, diesel engine 186-foot yacht he named the *Queen Anne.* In 1941 it was sold to the U.S. Navy, who renamed it the *Sardonyx* and placed on U.S. shore patrol. The Thayers built in 1938 a mansion on Bay Road in Miami Beach, Florida. Marjorie Bourne Thayer died in 1962 and, two years later, her widower married her sister, Florence Bourne, formerly Mrs. Anson Hard.

SAMUEL THOMAS (1840 – 1903), capitalist and railroad executive. Thomas, a brigadier general in the Union army, led the first black Union troops into battle. After the War he served as assistant commissioner for Mississippi during Reconstruction. He then entered the coal and iron business in Hocking Valley before becoming the leading contractor for the Croton Aqueduct in New York City. Thomas was president of the East Tennessee, Virginia and Georgia Railroad as well as a director of several other southern railways including the Central of Georgia. He was president of the Louisville, New Albany & Chicago and president of the Duluth, South Shore and Atlantic Railroads. Thomas moved to New York City in 1891 and eventually held controlling interest in Chase Bank. He gave $500 to establish a school in Thomasville, Alabama, a town named in his honor. He married in 1872 Ann Augusta Porter and had two sons and a daughter. Thomas died at "Agawam," his estate at Ardsley-on-Hudson. Among his children was daughter Eleanor who married Robert Livingston Beeckman, governor of Rhode Island. Thomas' grandson, Edward R. Thomas, owned the *New York Morning Telegraph* (which named the city "the Big Apple") and was the first American to kill someone in an auto accident. He married when she was seventeen Linda Lee, a Virginia beauty, who received a large settlement when she divorced Thomas then married composer Cole Porter. Her funds enabled them to live a high-profile life in society and their story was told in the movie "DeLovely." A granddaughter of Samuel Thomas was famed Miami society hostess Lucy Cotton Thomas whose sixth husband held the dubious title of "Prince Eristavi-Tchicerine."

HENRY BURLING THOMPSON (1857-1935), cotton manufacturer. Thompson graduated from Princeton in 1877 and in 1891 married Mary Wilson, daughter of Gen. James H. Wilson, the captor of Confederate President Jefferson Davis. He was president of the U. S. Finishing Company and chairman of the W. S. Finishing Company, as well as deputy chairman of the board of the Federal Reserve Bank of Philadelphia from 1916 to 1924. He was a director of the Equitable Trust Company and lived in Greenville, Delaware. Thompson was chairman of the board of trustees at Princeton and a friend of its former president, Woodrow Wilson.

EDWIN THORNE (1826 – 1889), leather merchant. A son of Jonathan and Lydia Corse Thorne, he was a brother of JIC members Jonathan, Jr. and Samuel and uncle of JIC member William Thorne. Reared as a strict Quaker, he entered his father's successful leather and shipping business in New York City and continued with him for fourteen years. In 1871 he bought Thornedale, their Dutchess County, New York, estate, consisting of 537 acres, from his father for $75,000 and spent considerable time developing a herd of Jersey cattle and a stud of trotting horses. Among his horses was a prize-winning three-year old named "Thornedale." His sister Phebe Anna Thorne founded The Society for the Prevention of Cruelty to Children. He was married to Charlotte T. Pearsall in 1857 and among their three sons was JIC member Oakleigh Thorne.

JONATHAN THORNE, JR. (1843-1920), tanner and merchant. A son of Jonathan and Lydia Corse Thorne, he grew up at New York City's Washington Square and attended the Quaker Haverford College. Thorne greatly increased his family's leather business which he sold in 1880. With his considerable proceeds he purchased land at Black Rock, Connecticut, and built "Schoonhoven." He also inherited part of Thornedale, the family's Dutchess County, New York, estate, and bred cattle there. His children were Dr. Victor Corse Thorne and Samuel Brinckerhoff "Brink" Thorne.

OAKLEIGH THORNE (1866-1948), capitalist. The youngest son of Charlotte Pearsall Thorne and JIC member Edwin Thorne, Oakleigh was a nephew of JIC members Jonathan and Samuel Thorne and a first cousin of JIC member William Thorne. He was head of the Trust Company of America and in 1907 asked JIC member J. P. Morgan for help in keeping his bank from closing after Morgan had already refused to save the Knickerbocker Trust Company (thus leading to the suicide of its president, Charles T. Barney). Morgan called upon fellow JIC members George F. Baker, head of the National Bank of New York, and JIC member James Stillman, head of the National City Bank, and the three collectively acted to avert the looming financial panic. Their actions would lead to their investigation by the U. S. Senate's Pujo Committee. In 1916 Thorne sold his New York City home to spend all his time at his estate at Millbrook, New York. Upon his retirement as president of the Trust Company of America he purchased the Corporation Trust Company of New Jersey for $500,000 so his valued employees would still have a position. Although a non-Catholic, he was a close friend of Cardinal Hayes of New York and in 1940 he gave to the church the Chancellor estate in Millbrook along with a sixteen-room house as a convalescent home for children run by nuns. Thorne married in 1889 Helen T. Stafford and they had two daughters. The elder married Birdseye B. Lewis and their son, Oakleigh, legally changed his named to Oakleigh Lewis Thorne when he was adopted by his grandfather. Oakleigh Lewis Thorne served as an aide to Admiral Nimitz in World War II and married Bertha Palmer of Chicago's Potter Palmer family. Among Mrs. Thorne's many philanthropic gifts was a painting by Eugène Delacroix given to the Minneapolis Institute of Arts. A son by Oakleigh Lewis Thorne's second marriage is historic preservation patron Daniel K. Thorne.

SAMUEL THORNE (1835-1915), banker and capitalist. A son of Jonathan T. and Lydia Corse Thorne, he married in 1860 Phebe, daughter of William Van Schoonhoven. Thorne was president of the Pennsylvania Coal Company as well as a director of several banks and railroads. He was a partner at the Thornedale estate in Millbrook, NY, and a champion cattle breeder. He and his family lived in New York City and at "The Crest" adjoining "Thornedale" in Millbrook. Thorne died on the yacht of fellow JIC member James J. Hill on the St. John River in Quebec. Among his children was Edwin who married Phebe Ketchum, niece of JIC member Franklin M. Ketchum. Their great-granddaughter, Julia Thorne, married Senator John Kerry, Democratic nominee for president in 2004, and was the mother of his two daughters. A Thorne great-grandson,

Landon Ketchum Thorne III, was a founding board member of the Jekyll Island Foundation and still remains actively committed to the organization.

WILLIAM VAN SCHOONHOVEN THORNE (1865-1920), railroad and corporate executive. A son of Phebe Van Schoonhoven Thorne and JIC member Samuel Thorne, he graduated Phi Beta Kappa 1885 from Yale and first worked for JIC member James J. Hill at the Great Northern Railway before became purchasing assistant to E. H. Harriman. Thorne then was vice president of the Pennsylvania Coal Company founded by his father, Samuel, whose father, Jonathan, was one of the chief developers of coal in the U.S. Considered an expert at railroad efficiency, Thorne was president of the Delaware Valley & Kingston Railway, president of the Island Railroad Company, and vice president of the Erie & Wyoming Valley Railroad. He was a patron of the Presbyterian Hospital of New York, the Society for the Relief of Orphans and Destitute Children, and the Manhattan Maternity Hospital. Thorne married in 1905 Julia Keyser and they had a son and a daughter and lived in New York City and in Millbrook, New York.

ALBERT EDWARD TOUZALIN (JIC member from 1886; died 1889), railroad officer. He was vice-president of the Chicago, Burlington & Quincy, and of the Atchison, Topeka & Santa Fe railroads, before becoming president of the Chicago, Burlington & Northern Railroad Company. He had substantial real estate interests in Omaha, Lincoln, and other western cities and was an organizer of the Nebraska National Bank. As an officer of the Burlington Railroad, in 1887 he led a group of investors

The Oakleigh Thorne residence in Millbrook, New York.

who purchased large land holdings, which he had acquired for $100,000, at Montecito in Santa Barbara County, California, for development. On the old Santa Fe Railroad, the first station out of Shattuck was named for Touzalin, known as "the Santa Fe's first super land salesman." He later lived in Boston. His daughter, Ellen, first married George Augustus Nickerson who died before 1910, and their daughter, Katharine Louise Nickerson, married Walter James, 4th Baron Northbourne. Their son succeeded his father as the 5th Baron Northbourne. After Nickerson's death, Ellen Touzalin married Rear Adm. Hon. Horace Hood, son of the 4th Viscount Hood, who was knighted posthumously after perishing at the Battle of Jutland. Their two sons succeeded as the 6th and 7th Viscounts Hood of Whitley. JIC member Charles Stewart Maurice named his youngest son Albert Touzalin Maurice in honor of Touzalin.

GEORGE EVANS TURNURE (1866-1933). A veteran of the Spanish-American War, Turnure married Elizabeth Gardner Lanier (1870-1935), sister of New York City banker and railroad investor James F. D. Lanier. They lived in New York City and at "Beaupre" in Lenox, Massachusetts. Their son, George, Jr., was a highly-decorated aviator in France and was made a Chevalier of the Legion of Honor. He pre-deceased his parents in 1920 and they are all buried in Lenox, Massachusetts, along with the Turnure's daughter, Elizabeth, Mrs. George K. Livermore.

ALFRED LEE TYLER (JIC member 1888-1891), railroad officer. A son of Gen. Daniel Tyler, he was superintendent of the Macon and Western Railroad and superintendent of the Philadelphia and Erie Railroad. In 1872 Samuel Noble, representing his family's firm, visited the Charleston, South Carolina office of Tyler, who was then vice-president and general manager of the South Carolina Railroad. The two organized the Woodstock Iron Company and, in the following year, they built their first furnace on two thousand acres they purchased in Alabama. As the business and surrounding village grew, the owners sought to create a model city. Cottages were constructed for the workers with yards and gardens, streets were laid out and lined with trees, a company store was provided, and a farm was operated to provide food and diary products. Churches and schools were built, all as a part of this prosperous community. In 1879, a second furnace began production. The village remained predominantly an iron town until 1881 when a second major industry was added: cotton textiles. The wives and children of the ironworkers furnished the labor for the cotton mill. When application was made to incorporate a village called Woodstock, it was discovered there already was a Woodstock, Alabama. The founding fathers settled on the name Anniston, in honor of Tyler's wife, Annie Scott Tyler. On July 3, 1883, during an official ceremony, Anniston was opened to the public. The Tylers had a son, Alfred, Jr., who in turn had a daughter, Ann Tyler Deyo. She donated a parcel of family land to the city of Anniston to build their hospital.

HENRY HOBART VAIL (1839-1925), publisher and editor. A Vermont native, Vail served as a sergeant in the Union army after graduating from Middlebury College. In 1867 he married Minerva Hewitt, who died in 1895. Vail was editor-in-chief and vice president of the American Book Company. He prepared and edited

McGuffey's Readers which had an annual sale of 1.2 million copies. Vail moved to New York City in 1890 and retired in 1911 when he moved to "T'other House" in Woodstock, Vermont.

THEODORE NEWTON VAIL (1845-1920), capitalist and telephone pioneer. A native of Ohio, Vail studied medicine for two years and eventually held honorary degrees from Dartmouth, Middlebury College, Harvard, and the University of Vermont. He was Chairman of the Board of Directors of AT&T and a director of First National Bank headed by JIC member George Baker. He retired from AT&T in 1890 and moved to his 3,500 acre farm near Lyndonville, Vermont, but was persuaded to return in 1907 during a financial crisis. Almost overnight he personally raised $21 million in capital and brought the company through its difficulties. In 1910 he engineered the purchase of the Western Union Telegraph Company for $30 million and served as its president for four years. Vail married in 1907 Mabel Sanderson and had one son, Davis Vail, who was a law student at Harvard. He also adopted his brother's daughter, Katherine Vail, who married in 1913 Arthur A. Marsters, secretary of AT&T. Katherine Vail was one of the founders of Bennington College in Vermont. Among her three children was Theodore Newton Vail Marsters. A nephew, James Vail Converse, was the first husband of Thelma Morgan, twin of the senior Gloria Vanderbilt. As Viscountess Furness, Thelma was the mistress of the Prince of Wales (later King Edward VIII) who unwisely asked her friend, Wallis Simpson, to take care of him while she was out of the country. Theodore Vail died shortly after arriving at Johns Hopkins Hospital from Jekyll Island in his private rail car.

Top: The first transcontinental telephone call was placed from Jekyll Island to San Francisco in 1915, with Theodore Vail on the far right with William Rockefeller next to him and J. P. Morgan, Jr. behind.

Bottom: The New York end of the call with Alexander Graham Bell seated in the middle (note Theodore Vail's portrait behind Bell). Bell's famous assistant, Watson, was in San Francisco with President Woodrow Wilson on the line in Washington.

WILLIAM KISSAM VANDERBILT (1849-1920), capitalist. A son of William Henry Vanderbilt and a grandson of the commodore, "Willie K." followed the family business by serving as a railroad president and director. He and his elder brother, Cornelius II, shared control of their huge railroad empire. After Cornelius II's death in 1899, Willie K. became the head of the family enterprises and sided with JIC member J. P. Morgan in some of the largest industrial consolidations in America, including United States Steel, of which he was a director. When he consolidated the two main Vanderbilt railroads, the New York Central and the Lake Shore, he increased the family fortune by $ 50 million. In 1875 he married an ambitious Alabamian, Alva Smith, who catapulted her husband's family into New York society through her own fortitude and sheer force of will, eventually forcing the imperious Mrs. Astor to include the Vanderbilts on her invitation lists. Alva was not fond of Jekyll, finding it not as social a retreat as she would have liked. Willie K. owned two lavish yachts, the *Alva* and the *Valiant,* and built a Newport mansion, "Marble House," for a cost of $11 million in 1892. They had two sons, W. K., Jr. and Harold, and a daughter, Consuelo, named for her godmother, the American-born Duchess of Manchester (whose brother was married to Alva's sister). Alva forced her daughter in 1895 to marry the 9th Duke of Marlborough in the most spectacular of the "titles for dollars" alliances of the era. The bride covered her face with veils to hide her tears on their wedding day, but the groom received a marriage settlement of $2.5 million in railroad stock with a guaranteed minimum annual yield of four percent for life. The Vanderbilts also built a million dollar

Consuelo Vanderbilt, who in a lavish New York wedding in 1895 married the 9th Duke of Marlborough. She was forced by her mother to marry and wore a veil to cover her tears.

Top left: Consuelo's mother, Alva, who risked social ostracism by divorcing Willie K. Vanderbilt and marrying O. H. P. Belmont. She is costumed here as Tosca for the Bradley Martin Ball of 1897. She later helped her daughter obtain an annulment so she could marry again; the Duke wed another American at the Paris home of Jekyll member Eugene Higgins.

Bottom left: Willie K. Vanderbilt, Jr. was an early automobile enthusiast. In 1904 he broke the world's one-mile speed record at Ormond Beach, Florida, covering a mile in just 39 seconds at 92 miles per hour. He traded his 250-foot yacht in 1925 for Fisher's Island in Florida.

Right: Blenheim Palace in England where Consuelo Vanderbilt reigned as Duchess. The marriage was estimated to cost the Vanderbilts $15 million dollars, including extensive renovations at Blenheim where the Prince of Wales (later King Edward VII) was a frequent guest.

town house in London's Curzon Street for the pair and, with repairs to Blenheim Palace, an estimated $15 million was spent in order for Consuelo to be a duchess. Consuelo was a great beauty, with a face compelling enough to cause the playwright Sir James Barrie, author of *Peter Pan*, to write, "I would stand all day in the street to see Consuelo Marlborough get into her carriage." The couple became close to King Edward VII and often entertained him at Blenheim but they were intensely unhappy. Both had affairs even though she produced two sons ("the heir and the spare"), separated in 1906 and divorced in 1920, one year before the duke married his second American wife. Willie K. and Alva divorced in 1895 and she married O. H. P. Belmont, five years younger than she, who had been a frequent guest on the Vanderbilts' yachts. Alva became a staunch suffragist (she was fond of saying, "Just pray to God. She will help you.") and, perhaps to atone for forcing Consuelo to marry the duke, helped her daughter obtain a Papal annulment of her marriage. Consuelo was then free to marry the French aviator Jacques Balsan, with whom she had a long and happy marriage. At her death in 1964, she was buried, at her own request, in the Marlborough family plot near Blenheim Palace where she had been such an unhappy chatelaine. Her father, Willie K., married in 1903, Mrs. Anne Harriman Sands Rutherfurd (whose daughter, Margaret, married in succession U. S. Undersecretary of State Ogden L. Mills, then Sir Paul Dukes, then Prince Charles Murat) and spent much of his time in France where he was a highly successful owner of racehorses. In later years, he lived at "Idle Hour," his Long Island country estate. When he died in 1920, he left a $50 million estate to his two sons, after having given $15 million to his daughter, Consuelo, and $8 million to his second wife.

ALFRED VAN SANTVOORD (1819-1901), steamboat company president. He began work in his father's shipping office and later built the first steamboat used for towing. On his *River Queen* President Abraham Lincoln and Alexander H. Stephens, vice president of the Confederacy, met in Hampton Road to discuss terms of peace. Van Santvoord married in 1852 Anna Townsend of Albany, New York. Among their children was daughter Katherine who married Eben Olcott, successor to his father-in-law as president of the Hudson River Day Line. Van Santvoord died on his yacht in the New York City harbor.

AUGUSTUS STOUT VAN WICKLE (1856 - 1898), capitalist. He graduated from Brown in 1876 and, as a young man, became president of two coal mining companies as well as president of his family's Hazelton Iron Works in Pennsylvania. He married in 1882 Bessie, daughter of millionaire Ario Pardee. They had a daughter, and a son who was born after his father's death. Van Wickle built "Blithewold," a forty-five-room mansion on thirty-three acres overlooking Narrangensett Bay in Bristol, Rhode Island, after buying on impulse in 1895 a seventy-two-foot steam yacht, the *Marjorie*, thus creating a need for mooring. Van Wickle died of an accidental gunshot wound while skeet shooting at the age of forty-two. His widow then married William McKee in 1901 and lived at their summer estate, "Blithewold," until her death in 1936. Her daughter lived until 1976 when the estate was willed to the Heritage Trust of Rhode Island, along with the furnishings and a $1.3

The Van Wickle gates at Brown University open only twice a year – inward at convocation to admit entering freshmen, and outward at commencement to allow seniors to exit.

Top left: The Walters Art Gallery in Baltimore, to which Henry Walters left his extensive art collection as well as one-fourth of his estate.

Bottom left: A beach party opens the 1901 season at Jekyll Island.

Above: Jekyll Island Club's tea house on Shell Road. Supporting structures throughout the island, including a power generating plant, were as extensive as those of many towns.

million endowment. The Van Wickle gates at Brown University, given by a bequest from him, only open twice a year – swinging inward at convocation to admit first-year students, and outward at commencement to allow graduating seniors to pass through. Van Wickle Hall at Lafayette University in Easton, Pennsylvania, was also a gift from him.

WILLIAM WARREN VAUGHAN (1848 -1939), attorney. After graduating from Harvard and from Harvard law school, Vaughn studied at the University of Heidelberg before receiving a Master of Arts degree from Harvard in 1874. His family lived in Boston and were summer residents of Northeast Harbor, Maine. He married Ellen Parkman and had two children: Samuel, a Boston attorney, and Mary, who married in 1916 Langdon Parker Marvin of New York City, private secretary for Hon. Elihu Root on the Alaska Boundary Commission, Harvard Overseer, and friend of Franklin Roosevelt.

HENRY WALTERS (1848 – 1931), capitalist. Born in Baltimore, in 1889 he moved to Wilmington, North Carolina, to manage his father's railroad. At his father's death in 1894, he was elected president of Atlantic Coast Line and transferred its headquarters to New York City where he lived with Mr. and Mrs. Pembroke Jones. After the death of Mr. Jones, who was known as "the richest man in the South," in 1922 Walters married his widow, Sarah "Sadie" Wharton Green Jones. Walters became the largest stockholder in Atlantic Coast Line Railroad and chairman of its board. He was an extensive art collector (he once purchased the entire contents of a palace in Rome that contained over seventeen hundred pieces) and yachtsman, frequently traveling onboard his *Narada,* and was a member of the syndicate that built a yacht to defend America's Cup. Walters bought the Louisville and Nashville Railroad from J. P. Morgan and was a trustee of the Metropolitan Museum of Art. He lived in Baltimore and at his Newport mansion, "Inchiquin," at the corner of famed Bellevue Avenue and Ocean Drive. The Baltimore art museum that bears his name was left his extensive collection as well as one-quarter of his estate. Walters also owned the original manuscript of *The Star Spangled Banner.* His wife's daughter was married to architect John Russell Pope, designer of the Frick Art Gallery and the Jefferson Memorial, whose connection with the Jones and Walters family secured many commissions for him, including "Villa Ospo," the Jennings family home at Jekyll Island.

ALLEN WARDWELL (1873-1953), attorney. A graduate of Yale and of Harvard law school, Wardwell was president of the Bar Association of New York City from 1943-45. He was a partner at Davis, Polk & Wardwell, a trustee of the Bank of New York, and chairman of the Red Cross Mission to Russia. Wardwell also served as president of the Juilliard Musical Foundation and of the Metropolitan Opera. He was active in supporting Russian emigres' after the War. He and his family lived in New York City and in Lawrence, Long Island.

JOHN ISAAC WATERBURY (1850 – 1929), banker. He was president of Manhattan Trust Company and served as a director of AT&T, as well as several railroads. Waterbury was president of the New York State Chamber of Commerce 1912-16, as well as a corporate director. He married in 1881 Elizabeth Moller and had three daughters. His grandson, renowned folklorist Dr. John Lorne Campbell, owned the Isle of Canna in Scotland and was president of the Folklore Institute of Scotland. He gave the Island in 1981 to the National Trust of Scotland and died in 1996.

JOHN GODDARD WATMOUGH (1837 - 1913), collector. He was a grandson and namesake of Col. John Goddard Watmough (1793-1861), a soldier and U. S. congressman who was a military hero of the Battle of Fort Erie during the War of 1812. The senior Watmough married Ellen, daughter of Judge John D. Coxe of Philadelphia, and had two sons who were naval officers, Pendleton Gaines Watmough and James Horatio Watmough. The youngest Watmough was a collector of paintings, armor, and Japanese ivories.

CHARLES NEWBOLD WELSH (1850 – 1914), author and editor. Born in England, Welsh was a reporter who came to America in 1895. He became an editor at the *Art Amateur* and was an authority on domestic science and juvenile literature. Welsh was a lecturer and author of several books. He married in 1884 Marie Josephine Loge' who died in 1908. Two years later he married Besse Denham. They lived in New York City and at Haverford, Pennsylvania.

SAMUEL PRICE WETHERILL (1846 – 1926), merchant and financier. Wetherill's family founded the white lead industry in the U.S. His father was president of the New Jersey Zinc Company of Newark, New Jersey, and invented the Wetherill furnace. In 1872 the son married Christine, daughter of George Northrop, a

Philadelphia lawyer. His home on the southeast side of Rittenhouse Square in Philadelphia was designed by Frank Miles Day. Wetherill's daughter, Christine W. Stevenson, gave the residence in 1915 to the Philadelphia Art Alliance, where it is still located.

WILLIAM DENISON WHIPPLE (1826 – 1902), soldier. An 1851 West Point graduate, Whipple served against the Apaches and Navajos as a colonel in the U.S. Army. He married in 1854 Caroline Mary Cooke and later served as a brigadier general in the Union army, including participation in the siege of Atlanta.

GEORGE WHITNEY (1885 – 1963), banker. A Boston native and Harvard graduate, Whitney was Chairman of the Directors of J. P. Morgan & Company. He married in 1914 Martha Beatrix Bacon, daughter of U. S. Ambassador to France Robert Bacon and JIC member Martha C. Bacon. He was chairman of the advisory council of Morgan Guaranty Trust Company and a director of General Motors. Whitney was instrumental in arranging an investment pool of $100 million to stabilize the U. S. economy after the 1929 stock market crash. He also arranged financing for the New York World's Fair of 1939-40. A director of many corporations, Whitney was also an overseer of Harvard and president of its board. He and his family lived in New York City and at Westbury, Long Island.

EDWARD KIRK WILLARD (1831 - 1921), broker. Willard was a member of the New York Stock Exchange. Although born in New York City, he was an early settler of Greenwich, Connecticut. Willard resigned from the JIC in 1888 and ten years later was expelled from the New York Stock Exchange for fraud.

Left: General William Whipple participated in the siege of Atlanta.

Right: Kermit Roosevelt and his wife, Belle Willard, were married in Madrid where her father was the U. S. Ambassador. Roosevelt would take his own life in Alaska while on active duty

JOSEPH EDWARD WILLARD (1865 – 1924), soldier and diplomat. Born in Washington, D.C., his mother, Antonia Ford Willard, was one of only three women to receive commissions in the Confederacy, having been appointed a lieutenant by Gen. J. E. B. Stuart as a reward for a daring night ride she made to warn Gen. Stuart's command of peril from the enemy. She married Joseph C. Willard, an officer in the Federal army, and they were Joseph E.'s parents. She was later imprisoned at the Old Capitol Prison in Washington, D.C., in 1863 for her alleged role in the capture of E. W. Stoughton by John Singleton Mosby. Willard's father owned the Old Willard Hotel in Washington, D.C.. The son studied at Episcopal High School in Alexandria, Virginia, then at the Virginia Military Institute and finally at the University of Virginia law school. He was an aide-de-camp to Gen. Fitzhugh Lee in the Spanish-American War, then was lieutenant governor of Virginia 1902-06, before becoming in 1913 our first ambassador to the Court of Spain. Willard used his personal fortune to protect U. S. dollars in Spain during World War I and at the outbreak of war he offered to resign and serve on the battle front but his resignation was declined. Willard was heavily decorated by the King of Spain, who sent his Ambassador as his personal representative to Willard's funeral. Willard owned the New Willard Hotel in Washington, D.C. He married in Baltimore in 1891 Belle Layton Wyatt of Middlesex County, Virginia, and they lived at Layton Hall in Fairfax, Virginia. She died in 1954, having had two daughters. Belle Wyatt Willard married Kermit Roosevelt, second son of President Theodore Roosevelt, and Mary Elizabeth Willard married the diplomat Hon. Mervyn Herbert of England, son of the 4th Earl of Carnarvon (Herbert's brother, the 5th Earl, was the famous excavator of King Tut's tomb). The Herberts' daughter first married Radu Tilea, the Romanian Minister to England, then married the Count Ledochowsky.

HOWARD WILLETS (1861-1938), commission merchant and landowner. Willets was a member of the New Jersey state senate from Cumberland County, 1875 to 1877, vice president of The Westchester Trust Company, and a partner at Willets & Company of New York City until his death. He was also a champion horse breeder. In 1898 he bought the two hundred and fifty-acre Gedney Farm of White Plains and added one hundred acres of adjoining land. He maintained on the property a famous herd of Jersey cattle and built his home there on a high point with a view of both Long Island Sound and the Hudson River. Willets imported "Bluebell," a full-blooded Jersey cow for which he paid $3,500 in 1904. Willets stabled his famous horses, "Heatherbloom" the jumper and "Hathaway" the racing champion, as well as sixty harness horses and thirty-five farm horses. Willets raised Dalmatians and claimed to have the largest kennels of Dalmatians in America, choosing "Gedney Farms" as his registered kennel name in 1904. He was the sixth president of the American Kennel Club. He bred "Heatherbloom," a dark bay thoroughbred gelding, which still holds the official horse show high jump record at seven feet-10 1/2 inches made at Richmond, Virginia, although he unofficially cleared an eight feet-two inch, and eight feet-three inch fence at "Gedney Farms." The property was subdivided and developed in 1913 when Willets moved to New Marlboro, Massachusetts.

THOMAS WILLIAMS (1856 – 1935), corporate officer.

Williams began in the lumber business founded by his grandfather. He became president of the White Rock Mineral Company and a director of the Guaranty Trust Company and other corporations. He built in 1922 at Carteret, New Jersey, bordering Staten Island, the largest mahogany sawmill and veneer mill in the world. Williams married in 1880 Emma W. Stott and lived in Lawrence, Long Island. His daughter, Edith Blydenburgh, gave to the Nature Conservancy in 1966 a farm and nature preserve at Smithtown, New York, in memory of her husband.

SAMUEL DEVEAUX WOODRUFF (JIC member 1887-1902). Woodruff's paternal grandfather, Walter Woodruff, was postmaster at Niagara Falls, while his maternal grandfather, Judge DeVeaux, was the founder of DeVeaux College in Niagara Falls, New York.

WELLAND DEVEAUX WOODRUFF (JIC member 1904-1920), paper manufacturer. Woodruff lived in Ontario and was a member of Jekyll's Game Committee. DeVeaux Woods State Park was established in 2000 in the northwest ("DeVeaux") section of Niagara Falls. The property was deeded in the mid-1850s as "The DeVeaux College for Orphans and Destitute Children" by Judge Samuel DeVeaux, one of the founding citizens of Suspension Bridge, New York. The college later became DeVeaux College, a military prep school, which closed in 1972, prior to being purchased in 1978 by Niagara University.

GEORGE WOODWARD (1863 – 1952), physician. Woodward was a member of the Philadelphia Board of Health, a member of the Pennsylvania State Senate from 1918 to 1946, and president of the Philadelphia Art Alliance. His home was "Krisheim" in Chestnut Hill near Philadelphia and he was largely responsible for the development

Top: The family of President Theodore Roosevelt at Sagamore Hill in 1903. Their second-eldest son married a daughter of Jekyll member Joseph Willard whose personal fortune protected American dollars in Spain at the outbreak of World War I.

Bottom: Theodore Roosevelt holding Kermit Roosevelt, Jr., a grandson he shared with Joseph Willard.

of Chestnut Hill as a residential area. Woodward married in 1894 Gertrude Houston, daughter of prominent railroad official Henry H. Houston. Among their children was son Stanley, who was the U. S. chief of protocol and ambassador to Canada.

JOHN WYETH (1834 – 1907), pharmaceutical manufacturer. Wyeth graduated from the Philadelphia College of Pharmacy in 1854 and began working for Henry C. Blair. He became a full partner with Blair in 1858 then sold his interests to open a drugstore in 1860 with his brother, Frank. The firm of John Wyeth & Brother prospered and Edward T. Dobbins became their full partner. John's only son Stuart became president of the company in 1907 and, at Stuart's death in 1929, Harvard inherited the firm until 1931 when American Home Products became its owner. The company is still in business as Wyeth and currently manufactures many pharmaceutical products, including estrogen replacement medicines for women. In addition to many prescription medicines, its over-the-counter consumer products include Advil, Centrum, Chap Stick, Dimetapp, Preparation H, Primatene, and Robitussin. Stuart Wyeth's ninety-six-foot steam yacht, the *Aurore II,* was purchased by the Navy and commissioned for service in 1917.

JEKYLL ISLAND CLUB HOTEL

Barclay Burns 06

The Jekyll Island Club Hotel is a world unto itself. This was true in 1886, when construction began for a hunting retreat on this beautiful barrier island for America's wealthy elite. Today, restored to its original splendor, it remains an exclusive, yet accessible, resort, offering all the amenities that its former incarnation reserved for the very few. Visitors now come from all over the country—and beyond—to savor the beauty of this historic treasure, designated a Historic Hotel of America by the National Trust for Historic Preservation.

The natural setting, of course, is an undeniable attraction. Situated on one of Georgia's pristine barrier islands, the lovely Victorian hotel is nestled among live oak trees adorned with Spanish moss. Protected from extensive development by the State of Georgia, the island has miles of beaches and maritime forests waiting to be explored. Wild deer, waterfowl, wild turkeys, and a variety of small game can be seen throughout the island, a sign that this place is shared by forest creatures. It is the perfect spot for peaceful, low-impact recreation and reflection—a place apart.

The Hotel is situated on the intra-coastal side of the island, near the Jekyll Wharf, where in 1888 millionaires began arriving aboard their yachts to enjoy the season.

Centrally located in the two-hundred-and-forty-acre historic village, the Hotel is an imposing structure, commanding the visitor's attention. Built in the American Queen Anne style of architecture, the Hotel features a distinctive turret, bay windows, and verandas, as well as superior views of the expansive lawns, the intra-coastal waterway, and the vast marshlands. Handsome interior details include Ionic columns in the dining room, twelve-and-fifteen-foot ceilings, oak wainscoting, and other handsomely detailed woodwork, as well as leaded art glass and distinctively detailed fireplaces.

No amenities are lacking in this wonderfully restored Victorian treasure. Gracious accommodations await the visitor, with 157 rooms and suites in five historic settings. Reminiscent of choices a century ago, today's guests may choose from the Clubhouse (main hotel), the Annex, and Sans Souci. The addition of two magnificently restored Historic District cottages—Crane Cottage and Cherokee Cottage—have dramatically heightened the historic experience of a visit to the Jekyll Island Club Hotel. Offering twenty-three additional guest rooms and suites, these luxurious "cottages" have become a part of the ambience of this lovely place near the sea.

Guests may choose from several attractive options for the

Jekyll Island Club experience, selecting from the wide variety of accommodations; enjoying an array of dining venues from elegant to casual/alfresco; and delighting in a buffet of activities designed for the visitor's comfort and enjoyment.

Recreation opportunities abound at the Jekyll Island Club Hotel. The Island's sixty-three holes of golf include the historic Great Dunes course, a true-ocean-side links course, along with three superb eighteen-hole layouts. Special winter season stay-and-play rates and inviting weather make golf irresistible year-round. Enjoy great tennis, too, indoors and out, including thirteen clay courts at the nearby Jekyll Island Tennis Center. You can even choose the indoor court built especially for J.P. Morgan. There's also a heated riverfront pool, regulation croquet greensward, resort putting green, bicycle rentals, charter fishing, and water taxi. Nearby are the Island's nature tours, water fun park, and outdoor performing arts amphitheater.

The Hotel has become the preferred meeting place for business, industry, and dozens of non-profit organizations. Meetings—both productive and memorable—are a tradition here. Whether you're planning an executive retreat for twelve, a conference for several hundred, or a gala wedding celebration with all of its attendant receptions and parties,

there is no place like the Jekyll Island Club Hotel. A devoted team of conference planning and catering professionals are at your beck and call, ensuring that all will go well and that, in the days and months ahead, your event will be a lovely memory.

Exploring Jekyll's absorbing history can be done on foot, aboard a motor tram, or horse-drawn carriage. Visit the museum. Or come inside Faith Chapel, where Louis C. Tiffany's stunning stained glass windows filter the sunlight. See the phone commemorating the first transcontinental phone call which was made from Jekyll. Stand in the room where the Federal Reserve Banking System was established.

The legendary Southern writer William Faulkner once said, "The past isn't dead. It isn't even past." Nowhere is this truer than here on Jekyll. History was made on this island, in this place. And it is alive and well. Arriving by private rail cars and yachts, Club members such as J.P. Morgan, William Rockefeller, and Joseph Pulitzer wintered here at the turn of the last century. And now, at the Jekyll Island Club Hotel, the season is yours; it's your turn.

Index of Jekyll Member Biographies

CREDITS

Library of Congress Prints and Photographs Division: 13 top & bottom, 14 right, 16 bottom, 19 top, 28 left & right, 33 top & bottom, 34 top & bottom, 36, 41 left, 42 left, 45, 48 left & right, 51, 53 right, 55, 56, 59, 60, 62, 65, 66, 69, 81, 83, 84, 88, 90, 93, 98 top, 101, 104, 106, 108 top, 111, 113, 123, 124, 126, 127, 129 left, 130 top, 133, 135, 138, 142, 143 bottom, 146, 149, 152, 153 bottom left, 155, 159, 161.

Courtesy of the Jekyll Island Museum Archives: 10, 13 left, 19 bottom, 20 left, 27 right, 41 right, 42 right, 74, 87 top right & bottom, 98 bottom, 103, 107, 114, 118, 121 bottom, 130 left and bottom right, 145, 151, 156 bottom left & right.

James J. Hill Reference Library: 19 right, 78 top & bottom, 137.

Corbis: cover.

Museum of the City of New York, The Byron Collection: 23.

Author's collection: 14 left, 31 top left & right, 39, 76 bottom, 94, 97, 129 right, 153 top left.

Time & Life Pictures/Getty Images: 108 bottom.

Miami University of Ohio: 31 bottom.

The Walters Art Museum, Baltimore: 156 top left.

U. S. Postal Service Archives: 53 left.

Ohio Historical Society: 71 bottom right.

Columbia University Health Sciences Library, Archives & Special Collections: 72.

The James Foundation: 87 top left.

Yale University website: 71 top & left.

Hoagy B. Carmichael: 46 top.

Alfred Scott: 121 top.

Robert Stokes: 76 top.

Stillman Rockefeller: 4.

Gerri Serianni: 143 top.

Mt. Washington Resort at Bretton Woods: 141.

Clendening Library, University of Kansas Medical Center: 20 right.

Georgia Power Company: 16 top.

Cody Country (WY) Chamber of Commerce: 24 bottom.

Original painting by Barclay Burns: 163.

Horace Holmes Photography: back flap author's photo.

Other photos in public domain.